The Young Voltaire

by

CLEVELAND B. CHASE

LONGMANS, GREEN AND CO.

55 FIFTH AVENUE, NEW YORK
39 PATERNOSTER ROW, LONDON, E.C.4
TORONTO, BOMBAY, CALCUTTA AND MADRAS

1926

COPYRIGHT, 1926
BY LONGMANS, GREEN AND CO.

MADE IN THE UNITED STATES

To
H. Y. C.

PREFACE

ONE cannot read Voltaire's prose without remarking its deftness, its rhythm, its color, its incomparable precision; few writers have possessed in a superior degree the gift of words. Moreover, to his contemporaries Voltaire was not primarily a stylist; they were moved even more by his thoughts than by the manner in which he expressed them. Yet now, except for a few of the shorter pieces like *Candide,* his writings have, somehow, the faded, dusty atmosphere of a museum. They are mummies; we can see what they were like, but life has left them. It is hard to realize what excitement, what ecstasy, they caused when they appeared. Those penetrating, incisive observations that set the eighteenth century agog with a forbidden joy are, to us, dull and commonplace. Voltaire seems to reiterate the obvious. We are vastly superior to him.

But it was Voltaire who taught us what we know. We are children of the second, or third, generation, disdaining in our self-confidence the riches that were accumulated by our illustrious ancestor. Voltaire was a teacher; his works, almost without exception, are didactic. Like all great teachers, he makes us feel superior to him because we have profited by his learning. It is true that he was always amusing; never did he allow himself to become dull or pedantic, but that was because he was a good teacher. He kept his pupils so entertained that they were seldom conscious that they were being instructed. Thus, to estimate the accomplishment of Voltaire, one must inspect, not what he wrote, but what he did. To grasp the genius of a man like Shakespeare one has but to go to his writings — comment and criticism are practically superfluous. Voltaire's own life was his masterpiece; to comprehend it one is to a large degree dependent upon the appreciation and the penetration of his biographers.

Just as Shakespeare's writings possess a different significance for almost every reader, so Voltaire's life is open to an almost infinite variety of interpretations. To capture on paper the essential qualities of his genius becomes a fascinating, if dangerously seductive sport. It is almost like that tantalizing childhood puzzle with which one attempted to roll ten little balls into one compartment; it is a simple matter to get half of them there, but to get them all in together . . . ! Voltaire's " spirit " has the illusiveness of quicksilver. One leaves the game more respectful, perhaps, but no less intrigued than when one began. And with Voltaire, one is kept in continual suspense by the fact that it is impossible to be quite sure whether one has been successful!

Few men have been as much discussed and as often written about as Voltaire. Were there a bibliography of the writings about him, it would include many thousand names. Almost every aspect of his life has been exhaustively studied. Volumes have been written about a single phase in his career; physicians, theologians, logicians, physicists, diplomats, economists have delved into specialized corners of his biography supplementing the endeavors of research students and literary historians; bitter controversies have taken place over the interpretation of a single passage in his writings.

Unfortunately, our knowledge of one phase of Voltaire's life is in direct contrast to this superabundance of material; the details of his visit to England are almost entirely ignored. Without exception his biographers admit those years to have been among the most important of his life, but, for the most part, they are content to pass over them with vague generalities. The first important step in the investigation of this subject came with Churton Collins' essay, *Voltaire in England*. Mr. Collins succeeded in gathering together most of the hitherto uncollected material about Voltaire's exile; many details that Mr. Collins missed, M. Lucien Foulet included in his admirable edition of Voltaire's English correspondence. In addition, M. Foulet's work is invaluable for the scholarly manner in which it throws light upon obscure and disputed points in Voltaire's exile. To both of these authors I gratefully acknowledge my obligations. These volumes, however, deal almost exclusively with minute details in Voltaire's exile; they make little effort to acquaint the reader with the general characteristics of that period as contrasted to the rest of Voltaire's life, nor do they attempt to show the exact influence of his exile upon the formation of his character. It is the aim of the present book to fill that gap. It gives the unusual and dramatic story of the exile, and attempts to trace the important part played by this episode and by other influences in the shaping of Voltaire's subsequent life and writing.

Voltaire's habit of denying the accepted beliefs of the world began early. He was an infant prodigy whose precocious ability was an accurate gauge of his mature genius. Upon reaching manhood, he did not cease to mature, to deepen, to develop his talents. But, as one might expect, the extraordinary amount of writing that he did early in life postponed somewhat his full intellectual development. For this and for other reasons, his outlook upon life did not crystallize until he was about thirty-five years old — or, to speak geographically, until he returned from his exile in England. It has always seemed to me that this residence in England is an important key to the understanding of the rest of his life. Those years witnessed the culmination of the varied influences of Voltaire's youth. He arrived in England talented but unformed, he left there essentially the man he would always be. Upon his return to Paris in 1729 he had forged the weapons with which he would carry on his battle with the oppressive influences of eighteenth century France. From then on the story of his life is less that of an individual than of a European influence.

It is with great pleasure that I thank those who have been kind enough to aid me in the preparation of this work. MM. Gustave Lanson, Paul Hazard, and Lucien Foulet graciously advised me in Paris while I was preparing the material for the book. Mr. Lytton Strachey, Professor Carl Becker, of Cornell University, and Professor Frank H. Ristine, of Hamilton College, were kind enough to discuss with me various problems that arose in interpreting events in Voltaire's life. To Dr. W. P. Shepard, of Hamilton College, I am especially grateful for the constant aid and encouragement that he has given me throughout the work on this book. I also thank the librarians of the Bodleian Library, in Oxford, the British Museum, in London, the Bibliothèque Nationale, in Paris, and Mr. J. D. Ibbotson, of the Hamilton College Library, who so kindly placed the facilities of their libraries at my command.

C. B. C.

CONTENTS

ILLUSTRATIONS

CHAPTER ONE
"THAT HATEFUL ISLAND"

CHAPTER ONE

"THAT HATEFUL ISLAND"

Elegant, austere, self-confident, seventeenth century Parisian society gave a single glance at the world outside of France and smiled depreciatingly. To the Frenchman of the *Grand Siècle* there were but three points on the map of literary history — Athens, Rome, and Paris. The rest was barbaric wilderness. Hot and furious were the quarrels between the *ancients* and the *moderns* — but the question which they debated was whether it would be possible for the glories of the past to be equalled. That there might at that very time be another order of learning and literary achievement worthy of consideration never entered the mind of the most radical thinker. The idea was inconceivable. Equally established was the French opinion that exile from Paris was the most drastic punishment which could be inflicted. To a Frenchman, travelling was " a disturbance of body and mind to no purpose whatsoever." As a natural result of this attitude a Frenchman almost never left his native country — and when occasional misfortune forced him to that extreme his one thought was of expediting his return.

With this point of view in mind it is easier to understand the opinion of England prevalent in France in the latter half of the seventeenth century. Spain and Italy, from their associations with Rome, were slightly known;

but England . . . ! Hated because of its religion, distrusted for its two revolutions, England was pictured as a desolate island, the home of uncouth barbarians. An example of the attitude then prevalent may be had from a guide-book published in 1654 by Father Coulon. In his introduction this seventeenth century predecessor of Baedecker says:

"Once the dwelling place of saints and angels, England is now the abode of parricides and fiends. For all that, however, she has not changed her nature; she still remains where she was, and as in the lower regions the justice of the Almighty is associated with pity, so in this hateful island you may observe at the same time the traces of ancient piety, and the commotion and the disturbance caused by the brutality of a people excited, spite of their Northern stupidity [*sic*], to the verge of madness."

That his book may not be entirely useless Coulon attaches the present to the greatness of Rome:

"Since in former days Julius Caesar had the courage and curiosity to embark from the shore of Calais in order to seek a new world beyond our seas, and to add to his empire provinces which nature had separated from our dominions by another element, our traveller need not fear to cross over to England, nor to trust himself to the winds and to fortune, which formerly brought that ruler of the universe in safety to the port of Dover."

A bit later he gives a significant last word of warning:

"I do not recommend any reader to penetrate very far into the country, for nature has subjected it to a very sorry climate, and placed it, as it were, at the extremity of the world, in order to forbid our entry. It would be better to set out once more for France." [1]

The French still pictured — for they were forced to rely largely upon imagination for their knowledge of that " new world beyond the seas " — they still pictured in England the tumult and the strife of the Arthurian legend. One traveller, in fact, was surprised to find that he did not have to fight a single combat at arms in going from Dover to London! It was as if a movie-infected European child should think that he could get on horse-back in New York City and ride out for a morning's buffalo hunt, with a few Indian skirmishes thrown in for good measure. French ideas of seventeenth century England were quite as ridiculous as this. Yet England had already produced, among others, Marlowe, Ben Jonson, Shakespeare, Spenser, Milton, and Bacon.

The English language was known even less than was the country. For what Frenchman would take the pains to learn it as long as French was, after Latin, the international language; when every English household had its French tutor, when Bacon wrote in French to the Marquis d'Effiat, and Hobbes in the same language to Gassendi? Saint-Evremond himself, although he lived a large part of his life in London and had among his friends most of the prominent Englishmen of the time, knew almost no English.

So convinced were the French of their own superiority that they were unable to see the slightest merit in another race.

[1] Coulon, *Le fidèle conducteur pour le voyage d'Angleterre* (quoted by J. Texte in *J. J. Rousseau et le Cosmopolitanism littéraire*, p. 4).

How long this condition might have lasted it is hard to say, had not Louis XIV, little suspecting the multiple consequences of his act, pronounced the Revocation of the Edict of Nantes. As a result of this, in 1685, sixty or eighty thousand Frenchmen took refuge in England, where they soon found political and religious sympathy.

With the exile of the Huguenots there begins a new and revolutionary phase of Anglo-French relations. Aroused by their exile, the refugees were naturally most interested in understanding the manners, customs, and political institutions of their new country. At their meeting place in the Rainbow Coffee House in London a group of them would frequently discuss the two countries. Historians, poets, journalists, antiquaries, translators of literature, science, and philosophy — their inquiries took in every field. They settled in London and entered wholeheartedly into the customs of the country; and, after discovering the true extent of English culture, they took upon themselves the task of supervising the spread of " English philosophism " in Europe. Although faithful to their adopted country, they still retained many connections at home, and were conscientious in relaying back their new and wonderful " discovery of England."

The discovery of this new horizon had rapid and widespread influence in France. Within a few years the popular attitude began to change. Books and pamphlets on many phases of English life and learning appeared. The papers and journals of Holland and England circulated widely. With the coming of the Regency after the death of Louis XIV, and the political alliance between the two countries, came connections between distinguished and educated Frenchmen and Englishmen. French society began to discuss English politics and philosophy; English Freemasonry was introduced into France and became a centre of liberal propaganda.

But this development of an anglomania would undoubtedly have been slow and feeble had it been forced to rely entirely upon these refugees — learned, but heavy and uninspired; inquisitive, but without insight into fundamentals; indefatigable workers who were unable to pull themselves out of the maze of their wide investigation to a position where they might get proportion and perspective. For the most part men of mediocre ability, they started the movement, and succeeded in attracting the attention of a number of able and distinguished Frenchmen to their new discovery. From this beginning grew the most significant influence of the eighteenth century in French politics and philosophy — the influence of England.

The first sign that the Huguenot journalists had actually aroused in intelligent members of French society a keen interest in England was the formation of the Club de l'Entresol. Founded in 1724 by the Abbé Alary for the discussion of ideas and institutions of various foreign lands, the Club de l'Entresol devoted most of its energy to the study of England. English journals and books were eagerly analyzed and discussed, private correspondents kept them in touch with the trend of English opinion, and English visitors to Paris took up in detail matters that had aroused the interest of these French explorers. It is known that Ramsay, Bolingbroke, and Horace Walpole were present at various meetings of the club. Doubtless other English visitors were glad to enter into their discussions. Until, in 1731, it was dispersed by the Prime Minister, Cardinal Fleury, for " meddling with too many things," the club remained the French centre for the dissemination of English political and philosophical ideas.

Starting with the formation of the Club de l'Entresol, each succeeding year witnessed new expressions of the rapidly growing curiosity about England. In 1725 came the publication of Muralt's *Lettres sur les Anglais et les Français;* in 1726 Voltaire left on his famous trip to England, two years later the novelist Prévost followed Voltaire; and in 1729 Montesquieu ventured a trip to England; finally, with the publication of the *Lettres Philosophiques* in 1733, the entire French nation became aware of its newly recognized neighbor.

From the point of view of keenness of observation and originality of material, the *Lettres sur les Anglais et les Français* by the Swiss Béat de Muralt is one of the most important of the many books upon England published in France during the eighteenth century. In it Muralt draws the contrast so often to be emphasized between the intolerant restrictiveness of French government and English liberalism. He is the first to use that overworked motif of eighteenth century philosophy, " English liberty." He remarks the vigor and integrity of the English as well as their stolid reserve and composure. The book is in the form of twelve letters, six upon the English, six upon the French, and the contrast between the two countries is brought home clearly. In those letters for the first time the French caught a glimpse of the true nature of England and of the English. Particularly striking to the French must have been such sentiments as, "There are people among the English who think more deeply and more profoundly than intelligent men of other nations." It is significant of the new attitude in France that this book of Muralt's was a distinct success in Paris.

Following closely upon Muralt's book came Prévost's novels, again indulging the growing taste of the French for an English flavor in their reading. Prévost, like Voltaire, was forced to leave France, and in 1728 he took refuge in England to remain there three years. On his return to France he commenced his famous *Mémoires d'un homme de qualité*. Twisting the plot of a novel to suit the demands of the book of travel which he was determined to write, Prévost was carried away by his enthusiasm for the English. "Few books," says M. Texte, "have done so much to create among Frenchmen a knowledge, to quote the author's own words, of 'a country which other European nations esteem less highly than it deserves, because they are not sufficiently acquainted with it.' And few writers have labored so earnestly to remove 'certain childish prejudices, common to most men, but especially to the French, which lead them to arrogate to themselves a superiority over every other nation in the world.'" [2]

Thus was the stage set for Voltaire. The propaganda of the Huguenots had succeeded in breaking down in the minds of many Frenchmen the ridiculous prejudices in regard to England, and in their place had left a curiosity about the realities behind the various myths and rumors concerning this strange country. But so far all that had

[2] Texte, *op. cit.*, p. 46.

been accomplished was the preparation of the French mind to be sympathetic to England. Before the publication of the *Lettres Philosophiques* it cannot be said that England had exerted any great influence upon France. The opening in the dyke of French tradition had been made. It was Voltaire who directed to this opening the flood of English influence.

Enraged by the insults of French society, Voltaire had fled from Paris in 1726, coming directly to the " land of liberty " of which he had recently heard so much. So cordially was he received by the English and so much did he like their institutions that he considered making England his permanent home. Two and a half years of exile, however, brought on an attack of homesickness, and he returned once more to the pleasures of the French capital.

On his reëntry to Paris, Voltaire discovered, perhaps to his surprise, that his interests were no longer what they had been before his exile. Then he had been content to enjoy the pleasures of that witty and superficial group which constituted French society, with scarcely a thought to such matters as the intolerant restrictions of Church and State. Formerly if he had discussed politics and philosophy it had been more to allow his superficial wit wider opening for a polished jest. Now they appeared to him matters of the greatest importance. The political freedom and the social tolerance that he had experienced in England had aroused in his inquiring mind an interest in these questions which he was never to lose. Wherever he went, whatever he did, upon his return to Paris he had always before his eyes the unpleasant contrast of

English tolerance and freedom, and the arbitrary intolerance of France.

Unlike the ordinary traveller who, for the short time that the novelty of his return remains, remarks the contrast of the new things that he has seen and who then sinks quickly into the routine of the life he had left, without an attempt at change, Voltaire was devoured by the significance of the differences between England and France. He was determined to bring home to the French the shame he felt when he contrasted with the institutions of his native land those of the free and vigorous England. He was intent upon shattering the smug complacency and self-satisfaction of his fellow-countrymen by the graphic portrayal of their frequent inferiority. Each of the books that Voltaire published during the years immediately following his return from England contained some example of the point he was making, but it was especially in the *Lettres Philosophiques*, published in 1733, that he brought England most strikingly to the attention of his compatriots.

The *Lettres Philosophiques* was supposedly an account of his impressions of England written by Voltaire to his friend Thieriot. In reality it was an open indictment of his native country addressed by Voltaire to all thinking Frenchmen. England he made use of by way of contrast. The facts that he brought out in the *Lettres Philosophiques* were not original; he drew his material from a thousand sources. But this raw material, put through the fiery furnace of Voltaire's genius, emerged rarefied and glittering, a work supreme in its field.

Short, terse phrases, epigrammatic sentences, incisive,

witty anecdotes gave the book an unrivalled conciseness and flow. The history of two centuries would be given in a sentence, a man's biography was written in a phrase. So compact were these letters that to a casual reader they might easily have seemed superficial, but seldom have so many striking thoughts been presented in so few words. The *Lettres Philosophiques* was a literary machine gun, each sentence a carefully aimed shot directed against traditional French indifference and bigotry. The staccato echo of the bullets resounded throughout the eighteenth century. Our analogy falls short only in that the sound of the shots from the *Lettres Philosophiques* was never monotonous.

The effect of the *Lettres Philosophiques* was astounding. Banned by the authorities of Church and State, the letters were eagerly sought after and discussed by all Frenchmen. For years their influence continued to grow. " Contemporary French readers when they had shut the book, found somehow that they were looking out upon a new world; that a process of disintegration had begun among their most intimate beliefs and feelings; that the whole rigid framework of society — of life itself — the hard, dark, narrow, antiquated structure of their existence — had suddenly, in the twinkling of an eye, become a faded, shadowy thing." [3]

With the publication of the *Lettres Philosophiques* the story of the growth of English influence in France is one of unchecked progress. Swept off their feet by the ideas so strikingly set forth by Voltaire, the French lost little time in investigating everything about this intriguing

[3] Lytton Strachey, *Books and Character*, p. 125.

island. Following in Voltaire's footsteps, a steady stream of distinguished Frenchmen visited England. English ideas and customs were rapidly taken up in Paris. By 1750 the movement had gone so far that anything from English lace to an English novel was assured instant welcome in France. The seed carefully nursed by the Huguenot journalists and sown throughout France by Voltaire had prospered and borne fruit.

Undisputed as is the influence of the *Lettres Philosophiques* on French history, some historians have been prone to discount the effect of Voltaire's trip to England upon the writer himself. They find in Voltaire's life before he went to England all the qualities that went to make up his tremendous influence. In this book we shall examine the trend of Voltaire's thought before he went to England, and the influence he underwent while he was there; by so doing we hope to be able to arrive at an estimate of his debt to England. In the meantime we shall have witnessed part of the intellectual development of one of the most fascinating men ever born; and have traced from their early stages several of the formative influences of our present civilization.

CHAPTER TWO
SCHOOL, PRISON, PROSPERITY

CHAPTER TWO

FOR some months following the twenty-first of November, 1694, in the parish of Saint-André-des-Arcs, in Paris, a tiny spark flickered on the verge of extinction; then hesitantly, sometimes imperceptibly, it gathered force until in the course of a hundred years it had grown into that irresistible flame which helped enkindle a whole nation into the white heat of revolution. It is curious to think that a man who exerted one of the most powerful influences our civilization has ever felt, was long expected to die in his cradle. Yet it is said that every morning for several months the nurse came down stairs to tell his mother that the child was dying. In fact it was not until Voltaire was nearly a year old that his family began to have confidence that he would live; while throughout the more than fourscore years of his life he had a bitter, unending struggle against ill health which he won only by his care for his body and his indomitable " will to live."

The story of his childhood and youth is as fascinating a tale of struggle against great odds, of bewildering success and humiliating rebuff, as has ever been written. What novelist could ask for a plot more replete with incident than the struggle of a young notary's son who, opposed by his family, successfully surmounts the walls of the most exclusive and most aristocratic society the world has ever known; who, at the age of twenty-five, is hailed as his country's greatest poet and playwright, is pampered by all society, and who can number even the king and queen among his friends? Yet such, in part, is the history of François Marie Arouet, later known as Voltaire.

When François Marie was born his father had an established reputation as a capable, reputable business man. He had continued the steady advance of his forebears, who in successive generations had been tanners, weavers, drapers, apothecaries, and purveyors, until at last he was in a position to look down upon the " low bourgeoisie." His income of 24,000 francs placed him among the solid, dependable men of the town; while his relations with such families as those of the Dukes of Saint-Simon, Sully, Praslin, Richelieu, and that of the Count of Moraiquiés, gave his household a certain air of distinction. He had drunk wine with Corneille, and the Duchess of Saint-Simon held one of his children at the font, with the Duke of Richelieu at her side. Voltaire's mother was of a family of slightly better social standing. Her father, in accordance with the customs of the times, had bought himself into the " noblesse de robe." But after all Voltaire's was still a bourgeois family with all the bourgeois ambition to push its way into the circles of the nobility.

Nor was such an ambition without chance of fulfilment. This was a time of social change when bourgeois with marked ability might buy their advance in rank without great difficulty. Each really successful man was able to place himself and his children either among the " noblesse d'épée, " or the " noblesse de robe." The two sons of

NINON DE LENCLOS

Corneille became officers, the elder son of Racine held an ambassadorial post, the son of a publisher became " fermier général." The records of the times are full of the names of men who made similar advances.

To do so had become an established convention. It was, then, in strict accord with tradition that M. Arouet should expect his son to take up the practice of law, with reasonable assurance of becoming " avocat du roi." Under ordinary conditions his expectations would have been fulfilled; but Voltaire's nature and the circumstances of his youth combined to give quite a different outcome to his life.

The influences of Voltaire's childhood, like those of most children, fall under the headings of family and school associations; and both influences were unusual. His mother, an attractive, witty, somewhat superficial woman, loved the brilliant and fast social life of the times. Among her friends were Boileau and the famous Ninon de Lenclos; while frequent visitors to the Arouet household were Caumartin de Saint-Ange, a perfect example of the ripe culture and brilliance of the nobility of the court of Louis XIV; the Abbé Gedoyn, one of the most distinguished Latin scholars of the age; the song writer Rochebrune; and the charming, corrupt old Abbé Châteauneuf, who claims especial distinction as having been the last of that long list of the lovers of Ninon de Lenclos. From early childhood the future Voltaire knew members of the three important classes of Parisian society — the " noblesse d'épée," the " noblesse de robe," and men of letters.

When Voltaire was seven his mother, who had long been in poor health, died, leaving the upbringing of this sickly, precocious child largely in the hands of fate. His father was far too preoccupied with his business affairs and his success to give more than a passing glance at him. His sister was quite taken up with the engrossing occupation of securing a husband; while his " Jansenist of a brother," as he was always accustomed to refer to his elder brother, Armand, was now, as always, most unsympathetic to all that interested Voltaire. The education of this young boy therefore devolved upon his godfather, the Abbé Châteauneuf. Abbé by name but libertine and freethinker by profession, the Abbé Châteauneuf was typical of that large body of nominal clergy who assumed holy orders merely for the livings which might be secured in that manner; and who were completely out of sympathy with the religion which they professed to represent. Debauched, cynical, yet withal witty and charming within the limits of his shallow society, the Abbé exercised a profound influence over his young pupil. Attracted by his precocious wit, he devoted much attention to the youngster, and from the beginning moulded his youthful mind in the direction in which his full-grown genius was later to follow. At the age when other boys were learning their prayers, Voltaire was being taught the *Moïsade* of J. B. Rousseau, an atheistic poem in which Moses figures as an impostor. In place of his catechism he learned the fables of La Fontaine. In all it was an extraordinary period of instruction.

When François Marie reached the age of ten it was decided to send him away to school. His brother Armand had been given over to the Jansenists for his education, and had come out fanatically imbued with their cheerless doctrines. As these doctrines were now becoming distinctly unfashionable, it was decided to give the second son over to the Jesuits at the Collège Louis-le-Grand. This school was attended by the sons of the most distinguished families of the realm, and the crafty old Arouet chose it with the purpose of thereby enabling his son to make friendships which would prove most valuable in his later life — a chance of which the son did not fail to make full use.

Of his relationships with the Jesuits, M. Lanson gives an admirable account. " For more than thirty years, up to the heated hours of the encyclopaedist battle, Voltaire's relations with the Jesuits were never broken. The latter were slow to give up the idea of winning over to their cause a man of such outstanding wit and ability; his disrepute among the Jansenists, to their minds, was greatly in his favor. And he on his side felt deeply indebted to such masters; in spite of all that separated him from them, in spite of his antipathy to the policies and doctrines of their order, even in spite of his own statements to the contrary when he was in need of proving a point, he really retained most pleasant recollections of Fathers Tournemine and Porée, and an affectionate esteem for the manner in which the Jesuits instructed the youths in their schools. He knew full well that he owed his good taste to them. He owed them his social self-confidence and finesse, he owed them his prejudices and limitations. So strong was their hold that he could never free himself from it." [1]

Fine teachers as they were, the Jesuits lacked the ability to implant any but an unreasoning morality and religion

[1] Lanson, *Vie de Voltaire* (Paris, 1906), p. 12.

in the heart of their pupil. To them religion was a matter of faith, of belief, and as such they taught it. Brought up nominally a Catholic, but at heart without a great deal of sympathy for the State religion, the critical mind of Voltaire did not absorb the truths advanced by his masters; they left him without enthusiasm. He was willing to argue, to weigh in his mind, but he could not bring himself merely to accept what was told him. Failing in this, most of the religious training of the Jesuits was lost to him.

The curriculum of the school consisted of a thorough training in Latin, and composition and elocution in French — little else. Slight though it may seem, this training was admirably suited to the development of Voltaire's latent abilities. It gave him a grounding in literature, and a constant practice in writing, both of which later proved most useful. Quick to discern genius in their pupils, the Jesuits soon realized the potentialities in this rather ugly, undersized little chap who had such keen eyes, and such a quick wit. He soon became a favorite of his masters, and had many pleasant relations with them. When the other boys were out at their games he was likely to be found inside in the company of one or more of his professors — discussing, arguing, questioning; making the beginnings of that remarkable fund of knowledge which he afterwards amassed. As one of his tutors afterwards said, " He loved to weigh in his little scales the great interests of Europe." A remarkably interesting, precocious boy.

In the regular course of his studies it was necessary for Voltaire to practice writing, especially in the field of poetry, where his ability soon attracted much attention even in the world outside of his school. Little of his work of this period has been preserved, but several well-known anecdotes shed light upon its character. On one occasion an old soldier, better versed in the ways of arms than in the intricacies of the pen, desired someone to write him a petition to the king requesting a pension. Because of his reputation, the task fell upon the young Arouet, and he produced a poem so deftly pleasing that it attracted the attention of the old king, Louis XIV — the best-flattered monarch the world has ever known — the soldier receiving his pension, and the young poet a great deal of notoriety. In fact, it is said by contemporaries that for several days following this incident he was one of the main topics of conversation at Versailles. Somewhat later he was introduced by the Abbé Châteauneuf to Ninon de Lenclos whom he so interested by his pleasing manner and witty sayings that she, upon her death soon after, left him a legacy of two thousand francs to be spent for books.

The Commencement Exercises at the end of the year at the Collège Louis-le-Grand were most fashionable events attended by all Parisian society. It is recorded that upon one of these occasions the number of prizes and rewards received by Voltaire was so great that he attracted the attention of the poet J. B. Rousseau, then at the height of his popularity, who insisted upon meeting the boy. He congratulated him amid the applause of all present and predicted a great future for the young poet. Following this incident the two were warm friends for many years.

It is easy to imagine that the impression created by his literary gifts would have a pronounced influence upon the young boy; and such was the case. When, at the age of seventeen, he left school he had made up his mind in favor of a literary career, and was prepared to stick to his decision despite his father's firm determination that he should become a lawyer. He realized his gifts, and saw in an exploitation of them the fulfilment of his hopes for happiness. He had the example of J. B. Rousseau to give him courage. Rousseau, son of the former boot-maker of the Arouets, had advanced to a position where his attention was coveted by the whole of Parisian society. He had achieved this solely through ability. Why, then, could not he, Voltaire, with influential friends, and perhaps equal ability, hope for as great success? Indeed it was a rosy picture — far preferable to that of bleak drudgery offered by a law office.

Not only had Voltaire determined upon a literary career, but he had resolved to become an integral and important part of the fascinating social life of the time. Already, under the patronage of his godfather, the Abbé Châteauneuf, he had been given a taste of what he might expect. He had been introduced into different salons, and had been welcomed in that epitome of the wit and debauchery of his age — the Society of the Epicureans of the Temple, better known merely as " The Temple." His school life had also fostered this taste. Personally pious as they were, the Jesuits were much more efficient in giving substantial training in good taste and manners than they were in instilling deep morality. When Voltaire left their care he was prefectly grounded in the manners and social conventions of the intricate society life of the courts of Louis XIV and of the Regency. This is a fact too often overlooked when we are surprised at Voltaire's subsequent meteoric ascent in society. When he finished school he had received the most perfect training then to be had in all of the social graces. He was prepared to take his place in any company without the slightest embarrassment.

At this school he had also made many friends among the sons of the noblest families, among those who would constitute the society of his lifetime, and he was determined to keep up these acquaintances. Poet he would be, but not of the proverbial type. Hunger, solitude, and complete abandonment to art — popular pictures of a literary career, then, as now — held no allurements for him. He would combine with his art the pleasures of society, making each coöperate for the advancement of the other, an experiment which would have proved fatal to many.

We have thus briefly sketched the major influences of his school life. We may already see the beginnings of three of his most characteristic traits. His literary ambitions, especially in the field of poetry, have been so encouraged that they assume a dominant position in his life. His early implanted dislike for the restrictions of dogmatic religion has been strengthened. And lastly he has acquired a firmly implanted love for the social life of the times, as well as the grace to acquit himself creditably in any company.

We now see the young Voltaire, seventeen, ambitious, and self-confident, step out into the society which he was to influence so deeply. His first years out of school were largely taken up with his struggle against his father. The latter was most determined that François should not ruin his life by giving himself over to anything as unsubstantial as a literary career. He was quite willing that he take his amusement in that way if he wished to, but to make a life work of it . . . ! His definition of literature is quite expressive of his views. " Literature is the profession of a man who wishes to be useless to society, a burden to his relatives, and to die of hunger." On his side the son was quite as vehement. The very thought of that disjointed, cumbersome mass which constituted the French law before Napoleon, was repellent to his orderly, logical mind. An answer to his father, long afterwards published in the *Dictionnaire Philosophique,* is quite as expressive as is the latter's definition. " A lawyer is a man who, not having enough money to buy one of those brilliant offices upon which the world has its eyes fixed (such as Counselor to the Salt Commissioners), studies for three years the laws of Theodosius and Justinian in order to know the practice of Paris, and who, being at last matriculated, has a right to plead for money if he has a strong voice."

Yet after all he was but a boy, without resources — and the Abbé Châteauneuf was dead. There was nothing else for it but the observance, at least superficially, of the dictates of this adamant father. For two years he combined with a desultory study of law as much of his beloved social life as he could get in. Much of his time was spent with his associates in the Temple where he " observed the decorums and practised the vices." He wrote much light poetry, and in general paid as little attention to law as possible.

In the summer of 1713 his father, tired of this unproductive struggle, decided on a new plan of action. François Marie was included in the party of the Marquis Châteauneuf, a brother of the Abbé, who had been sent on an embassy to the Hague. It is hard to tell whether the father thought by this means to start his son in a diplomatic career, or whether it was merely a means of getting him away from his Parisian haunts. At any rate the scheme was shortlived. Almost immediately upon his arrival at the Hague the young scamp proceeded to fall desperately in love with the daughter of a French refugee, Pimpette Dunoyer. His love was requited and for a short time the two lived in youthful ecstasy. But the end was not long in coming. The prudent mother, who had other plans in store for her daughter than marriage with the impecunious son of a Paris notary, soon discovered the situation, and demanded Voltaire's dismissal by Châteauneuf. The pen of Madame Dunoyer was renowned for its power in the destruction of reputations, and Châteauneuf thought it discreet to accede to her request. Accordingly, after a short delay, Voltaire was sent back to Paris.

His father, enraged by this new failure, refused to see his son, disinherited him, and even went to the extreme of getting out a " lettre de cachet " against him (which, it may be said to his credit, he never used). For some time after this Voltaire remained in hiding, finally purchasing reconciliation with his father by the renunciation of all that he held dear. He was to settle down this time without fail. Instead of continuing his former careless life as a student he became a clerk in the law office of a certain Maître Alain, living with the family and bearing as best he could the dull drudgery of his new life. Disillusioned in love (Pimpette soon forgot her vows of eternal constancy), and almost broken in spirit, Voltaire applied himself to his work.

This training in law, distasteful as it must have been to Voltaire at the time, stood him in good stead in his subsequent adventures in the field of business. Throughout his life Voltaire showed most remarkable ability in the management of his various business enterprises. Some part, at least, of the credit for this ability belongs to the training he received at this time. It developed, according to Desnoiresterres, " his perfect understanding of the intricacies of business, his clear-cut manner of thinking, his fertile administration of affairs, and the rare skill which he showed in the investment of funds and in the management of a fortune larger than any hitherto amassed by a single person." [2]

After some months of this sort of existence Voltaire found a new outlet for his ambitions. A friend intervened with his father, and he was allowed to leave the household of Maître Alain for that of the Marquis Caumartin de Saint-Ange, and by September, 1714, he was established in his new residence, far from his Parisian haunts. Saint-Ange was one of the most distinguished lawyers and business men of the time, and M. Arouet was quite willing that his son should have the opportunity of knowing him. Saint-Simon, often a severe judge, describes him as a man very capable in law and finance, honest, obliging, and

[2] Desnoiresterres, *Voltaire et la société Française*, Vol. I, p. 78.

polite. "He knew everything," he continues, "in history, in genealogy, in court anecdotes, and remembered everything he had ever heard or read, even to repeating in conversation whole pages." This man, intimately steeped in all of the history of the past three reigns, had a profound influence on the young boy, who, slightly conversant with the history of the ancients, knew almost nothing of the past of his own country.

Law was soon forgotten and Voltaire was satisfied to sit for hours listening to a personal relation of the inside history of the past hundred years. He learned of the lives and characters of the important people of the past through a thousand anecdotes, and received the benefit of Saint-Ange's great knowledge and ability in explaining the various political and economic happenings of this intricate period. The weaknesses of kings were depicted alongside of the whims of their mistresses, finances of states and of individuals were laid bare, the idiosyncrasies of individuals were shown in their relation to international affairs. The narrative omitted nothing. Saint-Ange loved to reminisce, and his young auditor revelled in these tales, so interesting and so important. Already his epic of Henry IV, the *Henriade,* and his great history, the *Siècle de Louis XIV*, had begun to take vague shape in his head. It was impossible that such a mind should let this chance go by neglected.

During the summer of 1715 the welcome rumors of the approaching death of the old king brought Voltaire back to the capital. This return was followed by a period of tremendous literary and social activity. The death of Louis XIV brought to the surface all of the subdued vice of the sombre days of his old age. In the frenzied turmoil of the reaction that followed we find Voltaire everywhere. We can see from his letters and verses of these years that he was upon a footing of equality and perfect familiarity with all the members of society. He was "le bel esprit à la mode," caressed by the ladies and made much of by men, supping with princes and composing impromptu verses in the different salons. He was a master of that very difficult art of making all kinds of remarks to his social superiors in such a manner as not to wound their dignity, but at the same time to place himself on a plane of equality with them. There are many amusing examples of his use of this faculty, of which the following is typical. Following the great success of his play, the *Oedipe*, the Prince of Conti wrote a poem commending the work. When the Prince read it to Voltaire the latter remarked, "Monsieur, you will be a great poet; I must get the king to give you a pension." The ability to say things of this sort was of great use to Voltaire in his intercourse in this touchy society.

In his will Louis XIV had left the powers of Regent to his illegitimate son, the Duke of Maine, but upon the old king's death his will was disregarded, and the Duke of Orleans became Regent. The natural result of this was the birth of a party of opposition centered around the dissatisfied Duke of Maine, and especially around his ambitious and scheming wife. This party, which had its headquarters at the Duke's castle at Sceaux, just outside of Paris, attracted many of the "beaux esprits," and Voltaire soon found himself a prominent member of the group. Among her various activities the Duchess inspired a large number of scurrilous and slanderous poems against the Regent which were eagerly passed around in the various Parisian salons. Voltaire being recognized as by far the ablest poet of them all, any poems of this nature which showed real ability, were generally attributed to him. It is impossible to be sure just how large a part he actually took in the writing of these things, but nothing seems more probable than that he gratified the Duchess of Maine by writing at least occasional satiric poems for her distribution. Whatever the truth of the matter may be, Voltaire was popularly believed to be the responsible person. Consequently, when the easy-going Regent was finally impressed with the necessity of taking some action in the matter, his punishment naturally fell upon Voltaire, who was exiled to Sully. But this was nothing very serious, and within a short time he was back in Paris again. The poems against the Regent continued, however, and two of the worst of them, one of which accused the Regent of the basest of crimes, were fixed upon Voltaire by a spy. This time he was sent to the Bastille. This honor, for little else could be considered the attention necessary to put him in this fashionable hotel for political prisoners, did not a little to enhance his importance. During his eleven months' stay there he seems to have been treated rather considerately, and he applied himself diligently to his literary work. He had already begun work on his *Oedipe* and now he put the finishing touches on it, and made very good progress on his epic, the *Henriade*. He left the Bastille on April 11, 1718, but it was not until October 12 that he was allowed to return permanently to Paris.

Before taking up the next great event in his life, the performance of the *Oedipe*, it might be well to glance at his social life during these years, and again we quote M. Lanson. "He frequented 'les companies les plus libres,' which are those where failings of one kind are offset by good qualities of another, at the Temple with the great Prior Vendôme, at Sceaux with the Duchess of Maine.

"At the Temple he met Chaulieu, the Abbé de Dussy, the Chevalier de Bouillon, President Hénault; at Sceaux, Cardinal Polignac, M. de Malezieu, Mlle. Delaunay. M. de Sully took him to Sully where he met the Duke de La Vallière and Mme. de Gondrin, the future Countess of Toulouse. He glided about like an eel in all of the places where vanity and pleasure found their fill: at Maisons in the home of the President, whose son was an intimate friend of his, at Vaux in the home of the glorious Marshal Villars and his attractive wife, at Paris and Châtillon with the banker Hoguère, where he found the poets Danchet and Crébillon and that adventurer Goertz, the meddlesome minister of Charles XII. We see him with Richelieu, in Poitou, keeping the young exiled Duke company, at La Source, near Orleans, with Bolingbroke, at Ussé in Touraine, where he found the jovial poet Grécourt, at Rivière-Bourdet in Normandy and rue de Beaune, Paris, with President Bernières. The polite Marquise of Mimeure is one of his friends; it is at her house that he has his first contest of wits with the blustering Burgundian, Piron. Mme. Ruplemonds took him to Holland; he spent ten days at the Hague with the poet J. B.

Rousseau, whom he had previously respected as a master. They parted deadly enemies.

"In poor health, often sick, and always thinking himself worse off than he was . . . at twenty the son of the 'payeur d'épices,' the clerk of Maître Alain, had put foot in the most brilliant society; at thirty he had forced the door of the court." [3]

He had at last "arrived," but his position was still far from substantial. He was getting too old to be interesting as an infant prodigy, and now was distinguished only by an ability to turn off verses at great speed, and by his pleasing personality. He had, therefore, combined literary work with his social activity, and, in the fall of 1718, came his first real test in this field, the production of *Oedipe*.

With supreme self-confidence he had chosen a subject treated by Corneille, in an almost perfect manner a comparatively few years before — but the reception given the play completely justified this confidence. The first night of *Oedipe* goes down in record as one of the most successful in the history of the French stage, and the play long remained popular. Although judged by the tastes and standards of today it is not a great play, to those who witnessed its first performance it seemed well nigh perfect. To those operatic qualities of the French classic drama which were so loved by the general public, *Oedipe* added enough spice in the nature of phrases with double meanings of political significance, to please everyone. Voltaire — it was about this time that he gave up the name of

[3] Lanson, *op. cit.*, p. 17.

Arouet for that of de Voltaire — was hailed everywhere as a fit successor to Corneille and Racine, and at the age of twenty-four was generally acknowledged as his country's greatest living playwright! *Oedipe* had a record run for those days, being played on forty-five successive evenings. The official censor (that dignitary who was so often to thwart Voltaire in the future) in giving his approval for the printing of the book said, " The public at the representation of this play promised itself a worthy successor to Corneille and Racine, and I believe that at the reading of it it will abate none of its hopes."

The poet used this first success in every possible way. He was always a master in the art of advertising, and *Oedipe* gave him all the chance he needed. He even succeeded in getting 1,000 crowns and a gold medal from the Regent — from the same Duke of Orleans who had put him in the Bastille a year before for a " literary " effort which he had falsely attributed to Voltaire! In all it is estimated that he received at least 4,000 francs from this one work, and a vast amount of publicity. If he had formerly been welcomed in all circles, his attention and presence were now everywhere courted. He was the hero of the moment.

CHAPTER THREE
THE IDOL OF THE COMÉDIE

CHAPTER THREE

THE IDOL OF THE COMEDIE

THUS did Voltaire achieve his first ambition. His bourgeois desire for money, jewels, pretty furniture, the acclaim of high society, and, above all, for complete social recognition had been fulfilled. After all, his early struggles with his father had not been about the results he was to seek in life; they were merely over the means by which this end might be attained. From the first both father and son had desired this social and financial success, this culmination of the steady plodding of generations of hard-working bourgeois, each seeking to rise a rung higher on the ladder of social success. Voltaire's steps had been more spectacular, less conventional, than those of his forebears, but none the less they were merely the fulfilment of bourgeois ambition. For the most part his energies had been bent upon the achievement of this ambition to the disregard of other things. He had moulded his thoughts and actions along lines that were sure to be fashionable. Therefore to understand his philosophy at this time we must know the tendencies of fashionable opinion during the Regency.

The Regency did not create libertinism, it merely added to it security and public approval; nor was eighteenth century deism a new discovery; its roots were deeply imbedded in the philosophy of the *Grand Siècle*. The seventeenth century had reasoned largely upon approved subjects. Theological matters such as the immortality of the soul and the knowledge of God had been declared *matters of faith,* and, as such, beyond the demolition of logic. But in the philosophy of the seventeenth century may be found many of the ideas that made its successor so revolutionary.; that the formal assertion of these doctrines was long deferred is due to the fact that conventions in modes of life and belief are harder to break down than they are in thought.

The new and revolutionary conclusions drawn from seventeenth century premises were given in popular form in the books of Bayle and Fontenelle. The latter, whose writings on scientific subjects became so popular that even society women were forced to take them up, eventually changed the ideals of culture affected by the conventionally correct. In the place of poetry and eloquence he substituted science. He made common property of the Cartesian system. He preached with withering logic the application of the principles of scientific reasoning to the problems of every-day life, discussing as a matter of course such forbidden subjects as religion and royalty. His use of historical criticism against the Church was a significant contribution to anti-Catholic theology. By separating the ideas of morality and religion, he made easier the tendency of his century to ignore them both.

The immediate effect of the pronouncements of Bayle, Fontenelle, and the others who professed this philosophy was to free men's minds from religious inhibitions. The sombre days of the old age of Louis XIV had tended to repress the instincts of the time for dissipation and the unrestricted pursuit of pleasure. With the advent of the

Regency all forms of debauchery became fashionable, and society used these philosophic sanctions to excuse its excesses. There was not a great deal of open antagonism to the Church. The attitude of thinkers and members of society was rather one of indulgent contempt and disregard. In the pursuit of pleasure it was less trouble for Philippe d'Orléans and his easy-going nobles to endure the formalities of religion, than to combat the elaborate machinery of the Catholic Church for the enforcement of orthodoxy. The Church, as a long-established institution, had its uses, but it was not to be taken too seriously.

In politics, as in religion, the prevalent attitude was one of passive criticism, rather than opposition. The disastrous end of the despotic policies of Louis XIV led individuals to examine state affairs. Vauban proposed tax reforms, Fénelon and Bayle denounced despotism and war, there was a keen desire for peace and personal liberty, but there was no general outcry against the established form of government. People merely wanted despotic powers to be limited.

" Love tolerance; hate persecution and civil war because of scepticism and fastidiousness; regulate life according to human nature and reason, that is, reject Christianity as unnatural; restore to the body its original functions and necessities; retain a certain amount of restraint in pursuit of pleasure through a wise desire not to overdo and out of consideration for the views of others; that is the substance of the matter put forth in the three quarto volumes which Desmaizeau published at Amsterdam in 1705. Pleasure-loving Parisian society carried it out in practice. Besides the generally avowed disbelief in religion, there was a tendency to detach from life all considerations of its ends and of supernatural sanction, and to give all attention to hunting and to earthly pleasure." [1]

The spirit predominant at the time is summed up in its entirety in a remarkable book, a mixture of fact and fancy. Whimsical and ironic, serious and joking, deft, bold, and spicy, the *Lettres Persanes* is an unsurpassed combination of logic and wit. With dry humor and irony these letters expose the thousand inconsistencies and injustices of the old régime. Members of society read them eagerly, admitted the justice of the tableaux, laughed, and went their way. The book epitomized their half-formulated complaints against the established order, but they merely shrugged their shoulders and continued their idle lives. The time for resentment and opposition had not yet come.

It must not be supposed that this new attitude was not revolutionary when compared to the staid orthodoxy of the seventeenth century. The enthusiastic reception of the *Lettres Persanes* shows what a striking change had come about. But up to this point the license and debauchery of the Regency were the only physical signs of the intellectual revolution. Before the new ideas could actually affect political and religious institutions, a great campaign of popularization had to be carried on. Before the full strength of this campaign could be felt, Voltaire had to be shown by personal experience not only the injustices of the old régime, but also the practicability of another

[1] For this quotation and general conditions during the Regency see Lanson, *op. cit.*, p. 26.

STATUE OF VOLTAIRE

system. The events which led up to his exile in 1726 cruelly impressed Voltaire with the injustice of the old régime. What he saw in England convinced him of the possibility of a government in which the balance of power between the people, the nobles, and the king kept each from oppressing the others, but left them all free to act for the good of the country. From that time on one of the main aims of Voltaire's life was to bring about the reform of the old régime along the lines of the English system.

In large part the influences that developed Voltaire's final political philosophy are to be found in a study of his life between the years 1726 and 1729, the period of his exile in England. In the years preceding 1726 Voltaire had become an integral part of the conventional social life of France; seldom after his return from England in 1729 did the superficial pleasures of society lure him away from his more serious interests.

In the preceding chapter we have seen the striking success which met his efforts to storm the gates of fashion. On the other hand, an examination of his writings during this same period will show, I think, that society on its side had succeeded in conquering Voltaire. His thoughts and reactions were those to be expected from a brilliant youth, ready to give voice to the more notable opinions of the members of his new circle, but he never ventured sentiments which might antagonize those whose favor he was courting. He included in his works enough philosophical spice to excite the interest of an audience always on watch for significant expressions of the new attitude towards Church and State, but the ideas he expressed were merely those that others had tried out with success. His daring was more apparent than real, and his allusions to matters of politics and religion were prompted by a desire to assure the success of the work he was writing rather than the exposition of new philosophic convictions. To estimate properly the significance of Voltaire's writings in this period we have merely to compare them to the general sentiments expressed in France during the years of the Regency.

With the exception of his epic poem, the *Henriade*, Voltaire's writing before he went to England was confined to light "society verse" and playwriting. It was in the latter field that he secured his most pronounced success, and it is to his plays and to the *Henriade* that we must go for information concerning his philosophy before his trip to England.

The audience that witnessed Voltaire's plays was ever on watch for remarks about politics and religion with double meaning which turned upon contemporary events and conditions. The preaching of the new philosophy had led individuals to take an interest in public affairs, but the absence of a chance for general discussion greatly hindered the formation of public opinion. There were no legislative assemblies in which the pros and cons of questions could be debated, no minority parties voiced their grievances, and, above all, there was no independent press to give public opinion a liberal basis for its judgments. In this condition it was the stage that fulfilled the function of a public forum. As M. Fontaine has pointed out, " In the theatre each night there was gathered an ardent, boisterous public, entirely at home in the theatre; it was not, as today, a fluctuating, everchanging crowd. There were heated discussions, not only on the merits of the play, but also upon contemporary events and rumors. It was there that famous men made their public appearance. There the heroes of the moment came to seek the applause of the populace and to enjoy their triumph — Maurice of Saxony after Fontenoy, d'Estaing after the capture of Grenada, the pirate Paul Jones after his bold exploits on the English coast. Did one wish to secure immediate publicity for some poetry, an epigram, or an anonymous satire, it was merely necessary to drop a few copies of it from one of the top boxes. They were immediately picked up, read aloud, and the next day were the gossip of Paris. The theatre seemed to open of its own accord and call for philosophy." [2] The success of a play depended quite as much upon the deftness of its allusions to matters of political and social interest as it did upon the literary quality of its lines or the cleverness of its technique. Good plays were hissed as being flat for their lack of political allusion; abominable plays were widely applauded for their daring attacks upon contemporary institutions. Writing under such influences, Voltaire would have been more than foolish to let slip such a chance to assure the popularity of his plays. One may rest assured that he did not neglect this opportunity. His plays were full of political allusion.

Audiences during the Regency took especial delight in the disproving of two traditional beliefs that had long been accepted as unquestionable facts. One of these was the divine right of kings, the other was the infallibility

[2] L. Fontaine, *Le Théâtre et la Philosophie au XVIIIe Siècle*, p. 8.

[43]

of the Church. Voltaire was assiduous in pointing out the fallacies in both of them.

How far Voltaire was sincerely interested in these attacks on the powers of the king and of the Church is open to question. Such passages were enthusiastically received by the audience for which he wrote, the writers and thinkers of the time gave him plenty of material from which to construct these attacks, and Voltaire took advantage of his opportunity. We shall inspect the significant passages in Voltaire's works during this period, quoting the most violent of his remarks about politics and religion, in an attempt to see just how far they reflect his own sentiments, and how much he is merely repeating things that he knows his audience wants to hear.

Limited as he is in the choice of subject by the rules of the French classical tragedy, time and again he devotes his plays to an analysis of the psychological reactions of kings. It is in *Oedipe* that he epitomizes the prevalent attitude toward kings when he says:

" *Un roi pour ses sujets est un dieu qu'on révère;*
    Pour Hercule et pour moi c'est un homme ordinaire." [3]

Here, as so often, Voltaire's " moi " includes the whole eighteenth century. He is indefatigable in his reiteration of this statement that kings, being mere men, are prone to all human mistakes and weaknesses, and that instead of being judged by the brillance of the crown they wear, they should be valued merely for their character and ability. In the *Henriade* he expresses this same belief in different words:

[3] *Oedipe*, Act II, scene 4.

" On a vu plus d'un roi, par un triste retour,
Vainqueur dans les combats, esclave dans sa cour.
Reine, c'est dans l'esprit qu'on voit le vrai courage." [4]

In *Oedipe* the king makes the following admission of his fallibility:

" Dans le coeur des humains les rois ne peuvent lire;
Souvent sur l'innocence ils font tomber leurs coups,
Et nous sommes, Araspe, injustes malgré nous." [5]

Far from the old idea that it was the subject's duty to die for his king is the statement:

" Mourir pour son pays, c'est le devoir d'un roi." [6]

This despoiling of the kings of their former prestige was merely the first step toward a more serious proposition. Once it was accepted that kings had all the weaknesses of ordinary men, it became evident that it was the height of folly to grant them absolute power. In both *Oedipe* and *Mariamne* Voltaire shows the tragic proportions that human weaknesses assume when they are backed up by the unlimited power of a despot.

In *Mariamne* he recounts the wholesale slaughter for most trivial reasons, the glaring injustice, the useless suffering, the criminal futility, of unlimited power in the hands of a man without self-control. In this play, Herod, choleric, undisciplined, and haughty, without insight into human nature and too proud to attempt to understand the mental machinery of those around him, falls violently in

[4] *Henriade*, Canto III, verses 47 *et seq.*
[5] *Oedipe*, Act II, scene 5.
[6] *Oedipe*, Act II, scene 4.

love with Mariamne. He marries her and tries by all the ruthless means he knows to conquer her. In a fit of jealousy he has killed her father before her own eyes; he has also killed her brother. His constant brutality, which makes him an abhorrent sight to Mariamne, is only emphasized by his occasional contrition and calmness. His crazed passions and his constant surrender to the whim of the moment, bringing in their wake widespread injustice and suffering, have made him hated and feared by subjects, courtiers, and neighbors alike. He is without a friend.

His wife, driven on by the fear that both she and her children will be murdered in one of his fits of temper, has prepared to flee from his court. He hears of her plan and vows to destroy her with her children, but upon seeing her he relents, and falling upon his knees he begs her forgiveness. At this moment the populace of Jerusalem, hearing of the plight of the queen, storms the palace to relieve her. Herod, believing Mariamne to be at the bottom of the conspiracy, orders her immediate execution. The palace, being cleared of the rebellious populace, the queen is executed. Immediately after her death Herod receives proof of her innocence, and falls into another of his fits of remorse.

The theme running through this ferocious melodrama is the danger of placing absolute power in the hands of an ordinary mortal. Herod is not entirely bad. His fits of remorse lead one to suspect that had he not possessed such despotic power he might have been quite a decent person. But his repentance always comes too late. His unrestricted power has made his slightest whim an irrevocable fact. The price of this is unhappiness and suffering on all sides, and among the most to be pitied is Herod himself. Realizing what his whims have cost him, he bursts into the following lament:

" *Quelle horreur devant moi s'est partout répondue!*
  Ciel! ne puis-je inspirer que la haine ou l'effroi?
  Tous les coeurs des humains sont-ils fermés pour moi?
  En horreur à la reine, à mon peuple, à moi-même,
  A regret sur mon front je vois le diadème:
  Hérode en arrivant recueille avec terreur
  Les chagrins dévorants qu'a semés sa fureur.
  Ah Dieu! . . .
  Malheureux! qu'ai-je fait? " [7]

Realizing his own culpability he says:

" *Non, il n'est plus pour moi de bonheur sur la terre.*
  Le destin m'a frappé de ses plus rudes coups,
  Et, pour comble d'horreur, je les mérite tous." [8]

Finally in a fit of despair he exclaims:

  " *Non: je suis un barbare, indigne de régner.*" [9]

How far removed is such a story from the blind worship of the king who " can do no wrong "! This desire to demonstrate the dangers of an unrestricted despot was especially welcome directly after the death of Louis XIV, who had held France in his tyrannical grip for almost a century. His injustices had not been as unbearable as those of some despots, but none the less France had

[7] *Mariamne*, Act III, scene 4.   [8] *Id.*, Act III, scene 4.
[9] *Id.*, Act III, scene 4.

grown restless under his domination. Voltaire in emphasizing these things was not saying anything new. He was merely repeating in a public forum sentiments which his audience uttered freely in conversation and which were generally discussed by contemporary writers.

The positive political philosophy of the period was, in general, that of the social contract: the king had been chosen originally by the people and should rule in their interest. The warring despot whose fame in battle was purchased at the price of the unhappiness of his subjects was condemned. Voltaire often reiterates these beliefs. When, in the *Henriade*, Saint Louis takes Henry IV to heaven and gives him instructions in the art of being the perfect monarch, he says:

> " *Qu'attentif aux besoins des peuples malheureux*
> *Il ne les charge point de fardeaux rigoureux.*" [10]

In another place Voltaire belittles the warrior-king, saying with a slightly superior air:

> " *C'est peu d'être un héros, un conquérant, un roi,*
> *Si le ciel ne t'éclaire, il n'a rien fait pour toi.*" [11]

When he speaks of the outstanding figure of the previous century, Louis XIV, Voltaire says that in the estimate of history his patronage of the arts will be considered more to his credit than the long and costly wars that he had carried on. Colbert is given a high rank for his financial reforms, while the prestige of great generals is neglected.

[10] *Henriade*, Canto VII, verse 434.
[11] *Id.*, Canto VII, verse 32.

These and other popular ideas which Voltaire promulgated were in the air during the Regency. He repeated them in his writings and, it is possible, had a fairly sincere belief in the truth of his words. But he was merely repeating abstract ideas. He had no great personal feeling about the matter. Intellectually he may have regretted the despotism of Louis XIV and the lack of freedom of the Regency, but actually neither these nor other contemporary abuses affected him. Whatever the abstract facts of the case may have been, the most significant thing to his mind was the fact that he, practically unaided, had been able in very short time to secure complete social and literary recognition merely because of his personal ability. To his mind faults which people might point out in a system that gave such recognition to ability, had been over-emphasized. He was more than ready to ignore them.

His confidence in the eventual justice of the old régime made him quite ready to forgive occasional mistakes. When the Regent kept him almost a year in the Bastille, and afterwards exiled him from Paris for some verses falsely attributed to him, Voltaire did not complain of the injustice of an arbitrary system that allowed such things. A few months after this incident his confidence was justified when Philippe made up for his former harshness by his generous treatment of Voltaire as the author of *Oedipe*. After the pension that he received at this time Voltaire is said to have thanked the Regent for the generous provision which he made for his board, but begged him not to bother himself in the future by providing for his lodging. A graceful joke, and Vol-

taire had forgiven and forgotten! Numerous incidents of
this kind made Voltaire quite willing to treat the shortcomings of the political system as unessential peccadillos.
There is a great difference between realizing that an
abuse exists and trying actively to combat it. If an abuse
does not directly affect us we may realize its pernicious
effect in theory. Morally we are likely to excuse it by the
thought that any attempt to change it is likely to create
a worse evil. Such was Voltaire's attitude. He had yet to
find out upon what beds of treacherous quicksand his pre-
tentious house was built.

Half-hearted as may have been his attacks upon the
existing system of government, Voltaire shows deep personal feeling in his attacks upon one political institution.
No one reading his writings of this period can doubt that
Voltaire was a pacifist. His dislike for the suffering of
war, his disgust at its utter uselessness, his hatred for its
fanaticism, are strikingly apparent each time he gets a
chance to mention the subject. And of all forms of war
religious warfare was by far the most detestable to his
tolerant spirit. He has pictured with vivid strokes the
horrors of the religious wars in France before the accession of Henry IV to the throne. The frightful details of
the massacre of St. Bartholomew sickened him. His sensitive being writhed at the thought of the wasteful carnage.
Throughout his life Voltaire was constantly changing his
epic poem, the *Henriade*, adding, deleting, rearranging.
The second canto is the only one that escaped this revision.
It is devoted to the story of the horrors of the massacre
of St. Bartholomew, and is written with the intense fervor
of unequivocal conviction. It is the only considerable

passage in the entire poem in which one feels that Voltaire is pouring out his own unqualified belief, and throughout his life he left it exactly as he had first written it. It is the expression of one of the most intense emotions of his early life.

One of Voltaire's most popular books, his history of Charles XII, is devoted to a practical proof of the utter folly of war. The life of Charles XII of Sweden is an example without equal of the colossal futility of war. Charles, one of the world's most inspiring examples of a capable, indefatigable ruler, in a life of self-denial, had but one fault. He spent his entire life making war. Starting his career at the age of eighteen with the successful defence of his kingdom against the combined forces of several of the greatest countries of Europe, within a comparatively short time he was complete dictator of Eastern Europe. Many times he overwhelmed forces outnumbering his own five or ten to one. Crowning and dethroning kings almost at will, his aims were usually altruistic. He sought always to be impartial and just. He undertook no offensive war with the intention of bettering himself or his country. Yet when he died he had done no lasting good. He had irreparably impoverished his own and other countries, and had wasted his great life, which might have been so productive of good to the world. In telling this most significant story, Voltaire impressed upon the world the terrifying uselessness of the thing he so hated — war. It is not too much to suppose that had Voltaire realized that his preaching against the old régime was to bring on the cruel slaughter of the French Revolution he would have restrained his tirades. He might have considered the old régime as it was a lesser evil.

So much for Voltaire's reactions to politics.

In discussing Voltaire's attitude toward religion, one must remember that the Catholic Church was a political institution of tremendous size and influence, and in France it was still firmly entrenched. As a political institution Voltaire, following the trend of the society he frequented, was openly hostile to it. As a religion he seems to have shared the indifference of his contemporaries to it. It may be that, just as he wanted to keep the old régime, after reforming it, he would have been willing to retain the Catholic Church, after divesting it of its political power, and correcting some distasteful influences which had crept into it. At any rate during this period his criticisms of the Church are inconsiderable when compared to the attacks that many of his contemporaries were making. *Ecrasez-l'infâme* was yet to be heard.

Voltaire is even more emphatic in his negation of the infallibility of the Church than he was in his denial of the divine right of kings. He received no such favors and pensions from the Church as he did from monarchs. He could speak with a clearer conscience. With a few minor exceptions his attacks are directed against the abuses that were so common in the misuse of the political power of the Church. A large part of the fourth canto of the *Henriade* is devoted to an exposition of the manner in which these abuses occur. Voltaire shows that for personal and political reasons the Pope helped one party in the civil war in France and called upon all those over whom he had influence to do the same. These people joined in the quarrel for religious reasons, bringing with them all the intolerance of religious fanaticism, so that in reality the Pope had used his religious position to help carry on a political civil war. In one of the many passages on this subject Voltaire exclaims derisively:

" *Sur les pompeux débris de Bellone et de Mars,*
  Un pontife est assis au trône des Césars;
  Des prêtres fortunés foulent d'un pied tranquille
  Les tombeaux des Catons et la cendre d'Emile.
  Le trône est sur l'autel, et l'absolu pouvoir
  Met dans les mêmes mains le sceptre et l'encensoir." [12]

In another passage he decries religious wars:

" *Et périsse à jamais l'affreuse politique*
  Qui prétend sur les coeurs un pouvoir despotique,
  Qui veut, le fer en main, convertir les mortels,
  Qui du sang hérétique arrose les autels,
  Et, suivant un faux zèle, ou l'intérêt, pour guides,
  Ne sert un Dieu de paix que par des homicides." [13]

Condemning the priests for their activities as political trouble makers, he says:

" *Ces prêtres, dont cent fois la fatale éloquence*
  Ralluma tous ces feux qui consumaient la France." [14]

Not only did Voltaire dislike the general idea of mixing politics and religion, but he especially detested the fact that during the civil wars in France the Pope had used

[12] *Henriade*, Canto IV, verses 180 *et seq.*
[13] *Id.*, Canto II, verses 17 *et seq.*
[14] *Id.*, Canto X, verses 392–3

his influence to get Philip of Spain to intervene in the struggle:

" *Rome, qui sans soldats porte en tous lieux la guerre*
Aux mains des Espagnols a remis son tonnerre." [15]

And again:

" *Philippe.* . . .
Soutient de nos rivaux la cause criminelle;
Et Rome, qui devait étouffer tant de maux,
Rome de la discorde allume les flambeaux:
Celui qui des chrétiens se dit encore le père
Met aux mains de ses fils un glaive sanguinaire." [16]

Such interference as this seemed unforgivable to Voltaire, and he causes the personification of Discord to say:

" *Du haut du Vatican je lançais les tonnerres;*
Je tenais dans mes mains la vie et le trépas;
Je donnais, j'enlevais, je rendais les Etats." [17]

Much as Voltaire revolted against the bloodshed and the useless waste of war, there was another feature of it that he detested still more. That was the manner in which it increased intolerance and, in the case of religious wars, fanaticism. Tolerance was Voltaire's titular god. He worshipped it and strove for its acceptance as some men worship their native land and others money. To Voltaire tolerance seemed the most important thing on earth. He was violent in his abuse of intolerant institutions or cus-

[15] *Id.*, Canto I, verses 101–2 *et seq.*
[16] *Id.*, Canto III, verses 347 *et seq.*
[17] *Id.*, Canto IV, verses 246 *et seq.*

toms; his greatest quarrel with the Church was over its intolerance. He did not believe fanaticism and religion to be necessarily coexistent, and he spared no pains in denouncing those who allowed them to be found together. Passage after passage expresses this aversion:

> " *Il vient, le Fanatisme est son horrible nom:*
> *Enfant dénaturé de la Religion,*
> *Armé pour la défendre, il cherche à la détruire,*
> *Et, reçu, dans son sein, l'embrasse, et la déchire,*" [18]

And again:

> " *Mais lorsqu'au Fils de Dieu Rome enfin fut soumise,*
> *Du Capitole en cendre il passa dans l'Eglise;*
> *Et, dans les coeurs chrétiens inspirant ses fureurs*
> *Des martyrs qu'ils étaient, les fit persécuteurs.*" [19]

He is just as vehement against the secular officials who stirred up the hated vice for their personal gain:

> " *Mayenne . . . sait combien le peuple, avec soumission,*
> *Confond le fanatisme et la religion;*
> *Il connaît ce grand art, aux princes nécessaire,*
> *De nourrir la faiblesse et l'erreur du vulgaire.*" [20]

With such abuses fresh in his mind, Voltaire takes care to impress upon his contemporaries his opinion that in many ways the Church had become degraded since the days of the early Christian martyrs. Formerly such faults

[18] *Id.*, Canto V, verses 83 *et seq.*
[19] *Id.*, Canto V, verses 101 *et seq.*
[20] *Id.*, Canto IV, verses 363 *et seq.*

had not been tolerated. He reproaches the eighteenth century clerics for their laxness, saying:

" *Infidèles pasteurs, indignes citoyens,*
  Que vous ressemblez mal à ces premiers chrétiens,
  Qui, bravant tous ces dieux de métal ou de plâtre,
  Marchaient sans murmurer sous un maître idolâtre,
  Expiraient sans se plaindre, et sur les échafauds,
  Sanglants, percés de coups, bénissaient leurs bour-
    reaux! " [21]

The monastic system also came in for its share of criticism. He did not like the idea of men hiding themselves from the world and its various problems. In the *Henriade* Voltaire speaks of the monks as follows:

" *L'Eglise a de tout temps produit des solitaires,*
  Qui, rassemblés entre eux sous des règles sévères,
  Et distingués en tout du reste des mortels,
  Se consacraient à Dieu par des voeux solennels.
  Les uns sont demeurés dans une paix profonde,
  Toujours inaccessible aux vains attraits du monde;
  Jaloux de ce repos qu'on ne peut leur ravir,
  Ils ont fui les humains, qu'ils auraient pu servir." [22]

So much for his criticism of the political abuses of the Church. There is much less material for the study of his reactions to the dogmatic side of the Church. The one thing he joins his contemporaries in criticizing is the implicit belief in miracles, and the superstition that crept into

[21] *Id.,* Canto VI, verses 125 *et seq.*
[22] *Id.,* Canto V, verses 30 *et seq.*

religion in that way. His incredulity is tersely expressed in a couplet from *Oedipe* which has often been quoted:

" *Nos prêtres ne sont point ce qu'un vain peuple pense;*
   Notre crédulité fait toute leur science." [23]

In another place he seems to warn one to beware of trickery in miracles, when Araspe says to Oedipe:

" *Ces dieux dont le pontife a promis le secours,*
   Dans leurs temples, Seigneur, n'habitent pas toujours:
   On ne voit point leur bras si prodigue en miracles:
   Ces antres, ces trépieds, qui rendent leurs oracles,
   Ces organes d'airain que nos mains ont formés,
   Toujours d'un souffle pur ne sont pas animés.
   Ne nous endormons point sur la foi de leurs prêtres;
   Au pied de sanctuaire il est souvent des traîtres." [24]

The passages that we have quoted give a general idea of the sentiments expressed in the books Voltaire wrote before he went to England. In politics he was content to follow the lines of least resistance. In certain passages he played up to the popular desire to lessen the prestige of kings; but Voltaire himself was satisfied that conditions continue as they were. His attack upon the Church was based upon his dislike of its political functions and especially a dislike of the Pope's interference in temporal matters. His attitude was more that of a reformer than a destroyer. In purely religious matters he expressed little criticism of the Church.

It has been generally supposed that, at the time of which we are treating, he had also definitely lost all faith

[23] *Oedipe*, Act IV, scene 1.   [24] *Id.*, Act II, scene 5.

in Christianity, and was confirmed in his deism. Several incidents occurred at this time, however, that permit one to question whether at heart Voltaire had actively abandoned the religion of his childhood.

One need not infer that he had lost all faith in the Church because his attitude toward it was not reverential. Flippancy toward the Church was one of the fashionable poses of the day, and Voltaire always took great care to be in style. Nor does the fact that he was undoubtedly lax, to say the least, in the practice of the Catholic religion, prove that underneath his external polish he did not still retain a certain amount of faith. It would have been impossible for Voltaire to associate with the society he frequented had he held himself strictly to the rules of the Church, and, as we know, the securing of a position in this society was the great aim of Voltaire's life at this time. There is no question of attempting to prove that Voltaire was still a good Catholic. The opposite of any such supposition is too obvious. What we should like to ascertain, however, is whether or not at heart Voltaire was at this time a convinced deist, or whether his final deistic conviction came as a result of his experiences in England.

A significant point in the determination of Voltaire's attitude toward religion is the nature of his criticism of the Church. The quotations that we have just given show that on the whole he criticised it from the point of view of an ideal religion. He still retained some of his youthful illusions, and looked upon the Church as an institution that should be a perfect instrument of peace and happiness. Each time that it fell short of this ideal he felt hurt. Especially did the political functions of the Church annoy him, for they did not come into the picture of perfection that he had in mind. It would seem that he still thought of the Church in more or less the same way in which he had been trained in his youth. Had his tendencies towards deism been fully confirmed his attack would have been from the point of view of dogmatic fallacy, and he would have devoted less attention to such relatively unessential matters as political policy. The significance of this attitude is much more striking if we compare it to his mature attitude toward the Church. In his mature years Voltaire constantly attacked it in matters of dogma. He applied the principles of historical criticism to the early history of the Church, and in so doing destroyed many long-standing beliefs. He justified the Church, however, in its capacity as a political institution. The Church, as a power within the State, seemed to him necessary, as was the family, and for that reason he justified its existence. This was his mature attitude as a nonbeliever. His early indignation with the Church each time it fell short of his ideal of perfection tends to show, one would suppose, that his opposition to the Church was not yet clarified. It was instinctive rather than reasoned.

Occasional incidents in his private life also lead one to the conclusion that he was not entirely confirmed in his deism. Voltaire, caught off his guard, at times shows signs of religious conviction. In 1723 he had a very bad case of small-pox and was expected to die. When he heard that he was in danger he sent at once for a priest and confessed his sins with apparently sincere contrition. Writing of this incident directly afterward he says: " I had him enter at once [the priest], I confessed my sins, and made my will, which, as you may well believe, was not long. After that I awaited death peacefully enough." [25] In this matter of fact statement there is none of the amused irony of the confirmed deist who has done something in which he does not believe. Voltaire has no apologies to make for his action.

His attitude seems to be rather accurately summed up in a letter which he wrote to Mme. Bernières in the summer of 1725. He does not believe in the Church; outwardly he is tempted to laugh at it; but deep down in his heart there is, as he says, " un petit vernis de devotion." [26] In short, his attitude was not far from that common to his companions of the Regency. Religion did not trouble him and he was quite willing to tolerate things as they were. He felt no immediate call other than to point out abuses which had crept into the Church through its interference in political matters. Centuries of Catholic training were in his blood; he retained a lingering, almost sentimental, attachment to this old tradition even after he had abandoned it intellectually.

It is not necessary to give here the details of these years of his life. They were largely a continuation of the years preceding the publication of *Oedipe*, only those years intensified. Throughout this period Voltaire was gradually undergoing a change from the flippant young courtier to the serious-minded writer. His literary efforts, which had originally been inspired quite as much by the

[25] *Correspondance de Voltaire*, Letter LVI, December, 1723 (translated).

[26] *Id.*, Letter LXXXIII, August, 1725.

MARIE LECZINSKA, QUEEN OF FRANCE

social prestige they would give him as by the desire to write, began to assume a more important position in his life. In 1719, when he was in exile at Sully, he divided his time between writing light, and, for the most part, inconsequential poetry, and social trivialities. He seemed ashamed to have it known that he could be really serious. For several years he attempted to keep up this pose, but he could not give himself up to it. His love of writing constantly distracted his attention from the serious pursuit of pleasure; and as time went on he found that his health could not stand constant revelry. After his escape from death by small-pox in 1723 he was quite serious for a year, and his letters show that he was often impatient with his friend Thieriot because he would not settle down to a sensible life. One can imagine the amusement this new attitude caused his former friends, who asked nothing better in life than the discovery of some new method of wasting time. After about a year of this seriousness he slipped back into the old life again, and seems to have been with his former friends quite constantly until the Rohan affair forced him out of society.

It was not to be expected that all of his literary work should meet the success of *Oedipe,* and *Atémire,* produced in 1720, was quite a failure, while *Mariamne* had to be rewritten before it was a success in 1725. He spent most of the year 1722 in advertising his epic poem, the *Henriade,* and in August, 1723, it appeared clandestinely. It had been disapproved by the official censor, and that action, then as now, added greatly to the popularity of its reception. How Voltaire was able to accomplish all that he did in these years is one of the secrets of his genius. He was constantly travelling and apparently wasting all of his time in the exacting rounds of social courtesies; but at the same time his literary output was nearly equal to that expected of a person who devotes his entire time to writing. By the end of 1725 he had completed and produced three tragedies and a graceful comedy, an epic poem that had been very well received, and over a hundred of those agreeable little poems, pleasing and often meritorious, in the production of which he remains master even to our day.

To complete our picture of his early life we may pass to 1725, and see the consummation of Voltaire's social progress — his entry into court. During the summer of 1725 the marriage of the young king, Louis XV, and Marie Leczinska took place. Writing from Fontainebleau in the fall of the same year Voltaire says: " I have been very well received by the queen. She has shed tears at a performance of *Mariamne*, and has laughed at *L'Indiscret*. She speaks to me frequently; she calls me ' my poor Voltaire.' " The queen was not only friendly to him in word, but in deed too, for we find that she gave Voltaire a pension of a thousand francs. The king also gave an expression of royal favor in the form of a pension of two thousand francs, while the Duke of Orleans had previously given him a pension of 1,250 francs. He was also in high favor with the father of the young queen, and counted the mistress and the secretary of the Prime Minister, two most important personages, among his close friends. Among the nobility he was everywhere welcomed with open arms.

His finances were in good condition. His three pensions

totaled 4,250 francs a year. He had received 4,250 livres income upon the death of his father in 1722. He had speculated widely and very successfully; including among his various enterprises the purchase of stock in the " Companie des Indes," the furnishing of supplies for the army, and the exploitation of a lottery. He had a genius for business and profited enormously from a majority of his ventures.

Pleased with himself and with life in general, Voltaire had little to complain of at the age of thirty. He had acquired a wide literary reputation; he was accepted everywhere as a social equal; he had already accumulated something of a fortune for a man of his age. Even if his country was not democratic, at least it was not hidebound. A man of ability was allowed to show his worth. In such a frame of mind we find Voltaire at thirty. Lulled into a feeling of security by his apparent acceptance everywhere, he was completely unprepared for the next incident in his life.

CHAPTER FOUR
LAUGHED INTO EXILE

CHAPTER FOUR

LAUGHED INTO EXILE

TOWARD the end of January, 1726, Voltaire was the victim of one of those unforeseen incidents which, apparently, insignificant, so often change the course of life and of history. He was at the Opéra, the center of a group of fashionable wits, talking in his usual self-confident, slightly overbearing manner. A certain Chevalier de Rohan, second son of a duke (who owes the recollection of his very name solely to this incident), dull and unpopular, and wishing to attract some notice to himself, addressed Voltaire in an insulting tone, " Monsieur de Voltaire, Monsieur Arouet, what *is* your name? " The stories of Voltaire's answer vary. They agree, however, in substance. Over-confident and proud, he answered an impertinent remark with an insult. According to one account he said, " I do not boast a great name, but I know how to honor the one I have," while another story credits him with having said, " The difference between our names is that I honor mine, while you dishonor yours."

A few nights later they met at the Comédie, in the box of the famous actress, Mademoiselle Lecouvreur. Rohan repeated his question, and Voltaire replied that he had given his answer at the Opéra. Sarcastic words passed between them, Rohan finally raised his cane threateningly, while Voltaire reached for his sword. At this tense moment Mademoiselle Lecouvreur practised one of the fine arts of the period and fainted, thus ending the scene.

Three days later came the climax. While Voltaire was dining at the residence of the Duke de Sully, he was informed that someone outside wished to speak to him. As he went down the steps toward a carriage which was in front of the house, he was seized by four lackeys, and given a thorough beating, while the Chevalier de Rohan, who was in the carriage, called out instructions to his assailants, among which was an injunction not to hit Voltaire's head, " as that is still good to make the public laugh."

Trembling with rage and indignation Voltaire returned to the dinner and recounted his experience. To his astonishment he received scant sympathy from Sully and his friends, who were inclined to find the incident amusing! An upstart, somewhat impudent bourgeois poet beaten by the lackeys of a noble — it was not a matter of great moment. The incident had transferred to life a scene from a Molière comedy; they laughed ironically at the ridiculous picture of Voltaire beaten by the servants. But to Voltaire, long accustomed to move on terms of equality in the most exclusive society, it was incredible. Cut to the quick he dashed about Paris and Versailles airing his grievance; but he found little sympathy among most of those whom he had considered his friends.

In other cases the instigation of similar affairs had been severely dealt with. For example, a rich Dutch Jew, Lys, had paid a lackey to beat up one of the violin players at the Opéra. The event had not taken place as the plot was discovered beforehand. Nevertheless the Parlement punished both Lys and the lackey. According to the letter of the law the Chevalier should have been punished by death! [1]

But here it concerned the Chevalier de Rohan. Few people wanted to incur the enmity of the entire Rohan family. And a cousin of the Chevalier, the Cardinal Rohan, one of the most important dignitaries of the royal household, had become interested in the affair.

Through the influence of Madame de Prie, the mistress of the Regent, Voltaire finally succeeded in having an order given for the arrest of " the men whom Monsieur le Chevalier de Rohan used in having the Sieur de Voltaire beaten." But the police were forbidden to enter the residence of the Chevalier in the execution of the arrest, and were also cautioned to proceed gently and so as to avoid all disturbance. Of course the offenders were never found. Thus this part of the incident was officially closed.

For Voltaire, however, the question was far from solved. He had himself spread the news of his insult far and wide, confident that his many friends would find redress for his honor. And at least, he thought, if they didn't punish the aggressor, the position of the offended man in society would not be affected. He soon found this far from true. Everywhere as he told his tale he met indifference, amusement. He had become the laughing stock of society. A new verb, *volteriser*, was coined, its meaning synonomous with *bâtonner*, to beat! Marias, in a letter of the fifteenth of February, says, " the poor *battu* shows himself as much as he can at court, in the

[1] Foulet, *Correspondance de Voltaire, 1726–1728*, p. 224.

city, but no one pities him, and those whom he thought his friends turn their backs on him." When Voltaire asked the Duke of Orleans for justice, the latter answered, "You have it." After having been received as an equal in the most exclusive society in the world, he found all doors shut! All because he had been the victim of an attack by a worthless noble!

What was the reason for this abrupt about face of Parisian society? Why was Voltaire so cruelly ostracised? There are apparently two factors in the question. In the first place everyone was agreed that Voltaire did wrong in taking offence at the original words of Rohan, and in replying to them with an insult. Had he passed them off with a laugh the matter would have been forgotten by the morning. But more important, it appears, is the matter of class feeling. Worthless as he was, Rohan was a member of one of the noblest families in the country; Voltaire was no one. It was a time of social change. Too many bourgeois were establishing themselves on a plane of equality with the nobles. This question became one of caste feeling. What might not happen if a nobody could insult a noble with impunity merely because he was a wit? "We should be unfortunate," wrote the Abbé de Caumartin, Bishop of Blois, and a constant visitor at the Sully household, "if poets didn't have shoulders." Whatever the merits of the case it would be a good thing to show this upstart poet that after all he was only a bourgeois. He was accepted by the nobles because they wished to be amused — he must not forget the fact. This, apparently, was the view of society.

The influence of the Rohan affair on the life of Voltaire, and upon modern history, can hardly be over-emphasized. The last fifty years of his life Voltaire devoted largely to his attempt to do away with abuses in Church and State. A large part of this attack was directed against the powers of king and nobles. Here it was that for the first time he came into personal contact with the abuses of the caste system. As long as he had felt that he was accepted at face value among the nobility he had not realized in more than a superficial way the deep-rooted evil of the system, the privileges of which he had hitherto enjoyed. Now, face to face with its injustice, he learned a lesson never to be forgotten. Aristocracy in this almost instinctive move in self-defence had started one of the most powerful of the various forces which produced the bloody Revolution and the downfall of the old régime.

After several weeks spent seeking redress through his friends, Voltaire realized that the only way to avenge the insult and repair his honor was to resort to the time-worn method of the duel. Accordingly, toward the end of February, 1726, he went into hiding and vigorously set about the mastery of this new art. For some time he was not heard from, and Paris speculated upon his whereabouts. Then suddenly he presented himself at the residence of Cardinal de Rohan at Versailles, where he had expected to find his adversary. The Chevalier de Rohan, however, had returned to Paris, and the Cardinal, aroused by this new impudence on the part of the poet, got out a *lettre de cachet* for his arrest. Again Voltaire was forced into hiding. Publicly beaten, baffled in all attempts at revenge, deserted by his friends, threatened with prison, Voltaire was in a pitiable condition. Again he set to work to perfect his mastery of the sword. Meanwhile he sent to the country for a relative, Daumart, who was to be his second. This action proved dangerous. The cautious Daumart, unable to dissuade Voltaire from his rash attempt, informed the police of his address and of his intentions, with the result that Voltaire was arrested on the seventeenth of April, and confined once more in the Bastille.

The captivity of Voltaire was not very rigorous. He was allowed a considerable amount of freedom and, everything considered, was quite comfortable. Maurepas, the lieutenant of police, writing to the governor of the Bastille, said: " His Royal Highness has instructed me to write you that the intention of the king is that he [Voltaire] have privileges and the liberty of the interior of the Bastille, in so far as they do not interfere with the security of his detention." [2]   He dined at the table of the governor, received friends, was allowed to read and write. In fact the number of people who came to see him became so great that the authorities were forced to issue an order limiting their number. As far as it went his condition was not unbearable.

As a matter of fact imprisonment was probably the best way out of the matter for Voltaire. There was no hope that he could get redress through his friends. He could not go back to his former life in Paris until his honor had been repaired. There was almost no chance of bettering matters by a duel. Even had he been successful in that, his condition would have been precarious. The laws against duelling were being severely enforced — the only penalty was that of death!

[2.] Foulet, *op. cit.*, p. 12.

But the Bastille was hardly a permanent solution of Voltaire's problem, and we soon find him making entirely new plans. Realizing the futility of remaining in France, he petitioned the authorities to be allowed to go to England, and his request was immediately granted. On the third of May he " was released from the Bastille and conducted as far as Calais, being allowed to go over into England, and forbid to come within fifty leagues of the court." [3] He was not formally exiled, but it was mutually understood that he was to go to England.

The introduction of the word *England* into this sketch of the activities of Voltaire comes with a suddenness that demands explanation. What prompted Voltaire to make such a radical move as this? Why did he thus voluntarily exile himself? The order of the king releasing him from the Bastille states definitely that he was to " leave Paris at once, and keep at least fifty leagues away, being unable to return without the express permission of the king. . . ." [4] There is no mention of leaving France in the document. As far as exile from Paris is concerned, it was the usual procedure toward those released from the Bastille. There was an expiatory period, usually short and lenient, before full pardon was granted — full pardon bringing with it permission to live in Paris. We have already seen that upon his release from the Bastille in 1718 Voltaire was not allowed to return to Paris for six months. Undoubtedly, had he wished to do so, he might have repeated his former experience this time.

But conditions were not what they had been before.

[3] *Daily Courant*, London, 3 May, O. S., quoted by Foulet, p. 27.
[4] Moland, *Oeuvres de Voltaire*, Vol. I, p. 308.

He had now aroused society and not merely a fickle, rather easy-going ruler. His crime too was more serious. Instead of a dubious charge of slander or treason, largely unproven, Voltaire had been overwhelmingly convicted before the bar of public opinion of the unforgivable crime of having been ridiculous. Simple toleration was no longer enough, and he realized it. He must do something to make people forget him and his sin. Nearly a year later we find him writing his friend Thieriot from England: " My services to those who remember me, but I hope I am quite forgotten." [5] Similar anxiety is shown in various letters of this period. The final proof of the validity of his reasoning is found in the fact that at his return home in 1729 everything had been forgotten, and he was able to resume his former position without embarrassment. It is very doubtful whether this would have been possible had he merely spent the conventional six months in the country.

Thus at the time of his confinement in the Bastille Voltaire had realized that some sort of exile was necessary. He had tried all other means and they had failed. What was more natural than that his first glance be toward England? As far back as 1725 he had been considering such a trip. Upon the refusal of the government to allow him to print the *Henriade* he had published a clandestine edition of the work at Rouen, but it was incomplete and mutilated — a mere ghost of the work he had in mind. He had been nursing the idea of bringing out in some foreign country the magnificent edition upon which he had set his heart. He hesitated between Amsterdam and

[5] Foulet, *op. cit.*, p. 90.

London, probably choosing the latter because of his friendship with Bolingbroke and with several other prominent Englishmen.

Voltaire had known Bolingbroke since 1722, and had been charmed with his breadth of knowledge and keenness of appreciation. Writing to his friend Thieriot after a visit to the exiled statesman at his home near Orleans, he says: "I really must let you know how enchanted I am by the visit I have made to La Source, the home of Milord Bolingbroke and Madame de Villette. I found in this illustrious Englishman all the erudition of his own country and all the politeness of ours. I have never heard our language spoken with more force or exactness.

"This man who has been immersed the whole of his life in pleasures and in business, has yet found means to learn everything and to remember everything. He knows the history of the ancient Egyptians as he knows the history of England. He is as conversant with Virgil as with Milton; he delights in English, French, and Italian poetry, but he delights in them with distinctions, because he is perfectly aware of the genius of each.

"After giving you such a portrait of Milord Bolingbroke, it will, perhaps, seem unbecoming in me if I tell you that he and Madame de Villette were infinitely pleased with my poem [the *Henriade*]. In their enthusiastic approval they placed it above all the poetical works which have appeared in France. But I know how much I must discount such extravagant praise." [6]

Since the visit mentioned in this letter Voltaire had not seen much of Bolingbroke, who had soon returned to

[6] *Oeuvres*, p. 35, Letter XXXV.

his English estates. However, friendly relations had continued between them, and Voltaire undoubtedly remembered Bolingbroke's enthusiasm for his poem when he was making his decision between England and Holland. It is also probable that the increased attention the French were paying to England aroused a curiosity in Voltaire to see this land about which there were so many conflicting reports.

Here was a chance to kill three birds with a single stone. He could leave France and allow his unpleasant notoriety to die down; he could give the *Henriade* a fitting publication; and he could inspect the intriguing land which had produced Bolingbroke, Falkner, Atterbury, and so many other of his friends. There was little on the Dutch side of the scales to attract him.

CHAPTER FIVE

VOLTAIRE DISCOVERS ENGLAND

CHAPTER FIVE

THE question is often asked, " In his mature years, what was Voltaire's ideal form of government? " He spent a large part of his long life and much of his tireless energy in combating the despotic absolutism of the France of his own day. His ceaseless tirades were one of the most important causes of the French Revolution and of the fall of the old régime. Yet it can hardly be denied that, had he lived to see the cataclysm that followed the misconstrued application of his doctrines, he would have thrown the full force of his vigor against the Revolution. One of his most firmly established convictions was that government should be for the greatest good to the greatest number, " government for the people." But to his logical mind, " government of the people, by the people," was silly sentimentality, unworthy of a moment's attention by one who would lay the slightest claim to the powers of reasoning. By what conceivable chance could one expect those stupid peasants of seventeenth century France, more like beasts than like civilized men in their thoughts and actions, people who plodded on in the routine of their daily lives, ploughing, reaping, eating, sleeping, with little more thought than the oxen they drove — who could conceive that these instinctive machines would be able to carry on the complicated workings of a great government as well as men who had been prepared by training and heredity for this express purpose? The faults of the system as it was were many and obvious. A despot like Louis XIV, who could plunge a whole century into misery and oppression, was a menace to civilization and should be curbed. The worthless nobles and the favorites who, like the insinuating parasites they were, sucked the life blood of the country were a plague to be wiped out. Intolerance and oppression were to be forever banished through pressure brought to bear by an enlightened public opinion. The old régime was to be kept, but first it must be given a thorough housecleaning. Above all, Voltaire required of a government order, tolerance, and freedom of personal expression. The means by which these advantages were to be gained seemed to him matters of minor importance, it was in the results that he was interested. Such, in general terms, was Voltaire's political philosophy. In large part the influences which caused him to adopt this attitude are to be found in a study of the period of his exile in England. The results from the political system in England under Walpole came closer to his ideal than anything he was to see during his lifetime.

In point of fact, seldom if ever in the history of our Christian civilization has there been such great intellectual freedom in any country as there was at this time in England. A combination of political and economic causes had brought about in society a condition of balance and sobriety. Everyone was glad to leave things as they were; each individual pursued his own course and was content to let his neighbor do the same. One might think anything, say anything, do anything as long as one did not actually interfere with the liberty of someone else.

The turmoil of the Cromwellian wars of the last century had inspired in the English a great desire for peace and political quiet. After those disturbing attempts at the imposition of religious conviction by force of arms, there was a widespread desire for tolerance and the freedom to worship according to one's conscience. The advent of George I assured the country of a monarch who would not attempt any despotic control over it; George I was much more interested in his German kingdom than in his British Empire. The power of the nobles had been controlled. The supremacy of Parliament had been established once and for all. The crushing of the Pretender in 1715 had entirely discredited the Tories. With the exile of Bishop Atterbury of Rochester they lost their only leader. At last Walpole was so firmly in power that he need fear nothing from political opposition. In 1724 there was but one division in the House of Commons. The accession of George II looked like a blow to Walpole, but George was ruled by his wife Caroline, who had resolved that there should be no change in ministry. Walpole was soon as firmly in the saddle as ever.

This combination of circumstances resulted in an unheard of state of freedom and tolerance. Religious and political persecutions were almost unknown. Quakers kept their hats on before the officers of the crown, even before the king himself, and Swift, who had a living from the State Church, wrote most virulent attacks upon the government. It was a period of great trade expansion. English ships were carrying English products all over the world. People generally were active and busy. Even the nobility was interested in building up the trade and the prosperity of the country.

Freedom of expression was almost unlimited. People were thinking for themselves, little hindered by convention and prejudice, and they said what they thought without constraint. As Voltaire, writing to a friend in France, says: " Reason is free here and walks her own way. Hypochondriacs especially are welcome. No manner of living appears strange. We have men who walk six miles a day for their health, feed upon roots, never taste flesh, wear a coat in the winter thinner than your ladies do in the hottest days: All that is accounted a particular reason [sic] but is taxed with folly by nobody." [1] And in another letter he says: " You will see a nation fond of their liberty, witty, learned, despising life and death, a nation of philosophers; not but there are some fools in England, . . . but by God English wisdom and English honesty is above yours." [2] " It is a country where people think freely and nobly, unrestricted by servile fear. If I followed my inclination it would be there that I would live, with the sole intention of learning to think." [3]

It was the England of Toland, Collins, Tyndall, Locke, and Newton; the England of Bolingbroke, Pope, Swift, and Congreve. It was a period when keen, clear, honest thought was in fashion. New discoveries, new theories, no matter how radical, were examined and judged on their merits. There was no biased condemnation

---

[1] Foulet, *op. cit.*, p. 61. The letter is not translated.
[2] *Id.*, p. 138.   [3] *Id.*, p. 45 (translated).

through fear of upsetting the "established order." Conventional England had made logical thought a convention, and proceeded to uphold its dictum with English thoroughness.

Could there be found anywhere a contrast greater than that between Walpole's government and the court of Louis XV? France, too, had had her religious wars in the seventeenth century, but instead of tolerance they had produced increased fanaticism and intolerance. The destruction of Port Royal in Voltaire's youth had been one of the many indications that the old spirit was predominant among those in authority. Lack of religious orthodoxy was still one of the greatest of crimes in France. Freedom of conscience was unknown. The government was an arbitrary despotism. The situation was aggravated by the fact that the king was weak. He was ruled by courtiers and mistresses. Injustice was often the rule, tolerance was unknown.

The nobility was made up for the most part of petty tyrants who passed their useless lives like dolls in a toy house around the court of Versailles. They prided themselves on their graceful idleness. Strutting about with toy swords flapping at their sides, they vaunted their titles and boasted with hollow arrogance of their lack of occupation. For a noble to indulge in commerce or do anything of use to his country was unheard of. The mere suggestion of such a thing would have been an insult to him.

Freedom of expression in France was largely limited to the right to flatter the ruling favorite. No book could be published in France without grave danger unless it had the express permission of an official of the king, and the most trivial excuse was used for the refusal of this permission. If a book mentioned a favorite of the day, but did not flatter him to his heart's content, its publication might be forbidden. If a book contained anything that did not appear to be heartily in sympathy with the existing institutions it might easily be destroyed and its author thrown into the Bastille. Incriminating inferences were drawn from the most innocuous statements and bewildered authors were put in prison where they might languish for years in ignorance of the accusation that had been made against them. The suspicion of having violated one of the many regulations of the king was sufficient grounds for punishment; proof was not necessary. Personal liberty was a myth in France. *Lettres de cachet* allowed people with influence to throw personal enemies into prison where they might lie for years with no charge brought against them.

The tyranny of the system was most pronounced in the realm of thought. New ideas and discoveries in science, philosophy, and theology were treated by the authorities as though they were pestilences about to sweep over the country. Every attempt was made to stamp them out with the greatest despatch. It was as if they had decided to stop the advance of time, and had declared that never more should there be anything new. The way of progress was over a thick barrier of laws, decrees, punishments, and prisons.

At the age of thirty-two Voltaire made the step from this stuffy hothouse of French artificiality to the clear vitality of English honesty. He had passed the time of life when one is usually subject to formative influences.

Under ordinary circumstances his opinions and reactions would have been definitely crystallized. But the disillusionment of the Rohan affair had come with the suddenness of a glass of ice water thrown in the face of a person asleep. Voltaire awoke with a start to find that the whole framework of his life had crumbled.

He was forced to rebuild from the bottom his entire life. Those things that he had taken for granted had proved false; defects that he had minimized in the régime in France had suddenly assumed tremendous proportion. Up to this point his life had sped along with unparalleled smoothness. He had confidently expected it to go on in that way forever. His confidence was now completely shattered. He was forced to change his estimate of values. Even if he were to obtain once more his former place in society, his life could not go on as before. The realization of the insecurity of his position would be a constant threat. His freedom, and his light self-confidence were gone forever. Thus, forced by circumstances to rearrange his estimate of values, Voltaire was in a mood to accept new ideas and a new attitude toward life. The striking contrast between England and France, coming into his life at such a time, made an impression on him never to be forgotten.

In the France he left there was nothing but inequality and hatred. Courtiers hated the provincial nobles, the *noblesse d'épée* despised the *noblesse de robe*, the newly rich envied and attempted to surpass the old families, they all despised the bourgeoisie, and the bourgeoisie despised the common people. In England he found mutual respect and cooperation between all classes. In France all his life he had been accustomed to see writers and thinkers, often starving, despised by society, and perpetually menaced by the arbitrary passions of the king. In England, at least until the advent of Walpole, men of letters had for years enjoyed a prestige greater than that of high birth; they were free to say and write what they pleased, and they had been widely rewarded with money and position.

Voltaire got to England in time to see the funeral of Newton. The spectacle made a lasting impression upon him. The great scientist was buried with honors that rivaled those paid to royalty. The greatest men in the kingdom vied with each other for the honor of being pall bearers. The country rose as a single body to bewail the loss of a man of such worth. Voltaire realized only too well that had such a man lived in France, not only would he have been refused any public recognition, but he would not even have been permitted to publish his works, and more likely than not he would have spent most of his life in prison as a result of the originality of his thoughts. Intellectual eminence had been given instantaneous recognition in England. Steel, Congreve, Locke, Newton, Gay, Parnell, Phillips, Addison, and other preeminent men had been rewarded with public office and independent means. In France the poet Crébillon and the son of Racine were starving, and J. B. Rousseau had been driven into exile.

It has often been said that England had no vital effect upon the character of Voltaire. Those who make such a statement profess to see in Voltaire's early writings the political attitude of his later years. They see in his disparaging references to kings his opposition to the abuses of the old régime, and in his attacks upon the political power of the Church the unquestionable proof of his deism. We have already seen that his attitude upon political matters was largely dictated by the desire to assure the popularity of his writings, and that he was not yet convinced in his religious attitude. He was still to feel personally the injustice of the old régime. If an impartial observer were to have hazarded a guess as to Voltaire's future character from his life before the Rohan affair, it is more than likely that his prediction would have omitted the essential points in Voltaire's life. To all appearances Voltaire was destined to be a wealthy and fashionable member of a most exclusive society, a very popular playwright, and a prolific poet. There is little in his life to lead one to expect of him such incisive works as the *Lettres Philosophiques,* the *Dictionnaire Philosophique,* and the scores of political pamphlets, or such histories as the lives of Charles XII and Louis XIV. If the same observer had attempted his prophecy after the publication of the works inspired by Voltaire's exile in England — the *Lettres Philosophiques,* the *Histoire de Charles XII,* and *Brutus* — he would have been able to make a very fair estimate of the future accomplishment of Voltaire. The two and a half years of his exile had left him indelibly stamped. His formative period was over. Henceforth his life was to be devoted to accomplishment. He left France a poet, he returned a reformer; but a reformer whose weapons were logic and wit, not force and ponderousness.

CHAPTER SIX
CHANGES OF FORTUNE

CHAPTER SIX

CHANGES OF FORTUNE

VOLTAIRE'S sojourn in England, so fascinating and so bewildering in its complexity, shows perhaps better than any other period of his life his tremendous capacity for work and his versatility of interest. Here we see him deftly and intelligently absorbing the entire culture of a foreign nation. He delves into out-of-the-way corners of history, philosophy, literature, and religion; he sees at first hand various social and economic forces at work; he gets to know the particular differences and foibles of all classes and parties — and at the same time he continues his own unending literary output.

It is doubtful whether a foreigner ever before got such an extensive and such an accurate idea of a country in so limited a time as did Voltaire of England. In a draft for one of the *Lettres Philosophiques* he gives us an idea of some of his activities. He speaks of himself as a private citizen " with leisure and perseverance enough to learn to speak English; who would talk freely with both Whigs and Tories; who would dine with a Bishop and take supper with a Quaker; would go on Saturday to a Synagogue and on Sunday to St. Paul's; would hear a sermon in the morning and see a comedy after dinner; who would go from the Court to the Exchange; and who besides all this, would not allow himself to be repulsed by the coldness and by the icy and disdainful airs with which English ladies begin every acquaintance, and from which some of them never free themselves." [1] Whatever his preoccupation, however great his innate partiality, Voltaire lost no chance to investigate the country he was visiting. As Morley says, " Voltaire was no dilettante traveller, constructing his views and deducing theories of national life out of his own uninstructed consciousness. No German could have worked more diligently at the facts, and we may say here once for all, that if it is often necessary to condemn him for superficiality, this lack of depth never at any time proceeds from want of painstaking." [2]

Before he could start on any of these varied investigations, however, it was imperative that Voltaire should have a working knowledge of the language. Had he merely desired to do the thing conventionally, his native tongue would have sufficed to meet almost all needs. A large proportion of the English nobility spoke French; Lady Bolingbroke could use no other language, and her husband was as fluent in one as in the other; the large colony of Huguenot exiles at the Rainbow Coffee House could have given him second-hand most of the information he required. But Voltaire would not be satisfied with this method, and his first act upon arriving in England was to withdraw to a secluded village, where he devoted himself to intensive study.

It is impossible to determine exactly what knowledge Voltaire had of English when he landed at Dover. [3] It

[1] Moland, *op. cit.*, XXII, 18 (translated).

[2] Morley, *Voltaire*, p. 81.

[3] Collins, *Voltaire, Montesquieu and Rousseau in England* (pp. 17, 18), takes it for granted that he was able to talk to people in English at the Greenwich Fair when he first landed, basing his conclusion on the

seems quite likely that Falkner, Atterbury, Bolingbroke, and other Englishmen whom he met in France, although they all conversed in French, inspired in him the desire to have at least a slight knowledge of English. It is possible that he was able to read, and perhaps to write English, before he decided to make the trip. When he finally decided upon the trip to England, Voltaire set to work industriously to learn the language. He tells us himself that while he was in the Bastille his friend Thieriot brought him a number of English books.[4] A recently discovered note-book which he kept during this summer (1726) shows that a month or two after his arrival at Dover he was using English in his private notes, and using it comprehensively.[5] It is doubtful whether this would have been possible had he not studied English previously in France.

Voltaire probably arrived in England in the middle of May, and seems to have remained studying in the secluded village near Dover for some two and a half months. Definite details of this period are missing, but we know from a letter of the twelfth of August that up

---

famous letter in which Voltaire supposedly depicts his landing at Dover. This brilliant letter was not written until some two years after his arrival in England, and is obviously a piecing-together of his impressions of England during his first two years there. When it was written, this letter was probably intended to be the first letter in the *Lettres Philosophiques*, but was not included in that work when it was finally printed. We can put no faith at all in the statement of individual facts in this letter. *Cf.* Lanson's edition of the *Lettres Philosophiques*, Vol. II, p. 256 ff.

[4] Beuchot, *Oeuvres de Voltaire*, XLVIII, p. 6.

[5] This note-book was discovered in the Imperial Library in Petrograd, and the text was published in *The English Review*, February, 1914, p. 313 ff.

to that date he had neither seen his English friends nor had he been to London.

In the first part of August Voltaire made a mysterious trip back to Paris. Writing afterward from Calais, on his way to England, he says: " I will confess to you then, my dear Thieriot, I took a little trip to Paris. As I did not see you there you may easily guess that I saw no one. I sought just one man, whose cowardly instincts hid him from me, as though he had guessed that I was on his track. Finally the fear of being discovered made me leave in more haste than I had come. . . ." [6] It may be that Voltaire's explanation of the trip, as a last attempt to find Rohan, is correct, but perhaps, as M. Foulet suggests, there was also a financial motive in the secret voyage.[7] When Voltaire left the Bastille he had with him thirteen hundred francs in gold. This was enough for a short visit to England, but if the trip were to be prolonged for several years he would need more. It seems more than likely that one of the prime motives for the expedition was Voltaire's desire to see his agent, Dubreuil, that he might put his financial affairs in order.

Whatever the motives for this trip may have been, Voltaire was back in England by the middle of August, and this time he went directly to London. His introduction to the English capital was of the most dismal nature. The letter in which he describes his arrival, one of the first examples we possess of Voltaire's ability to handle English, is touchingly pathetic: " I came into England . . . very much dissatisfied with my secret voiage into

---

[6] Moland, *op. cit.*, Vol. XXXIII, Letter 165 (translated).
[7] Foulet, *op. cit.*, p. 44, n.

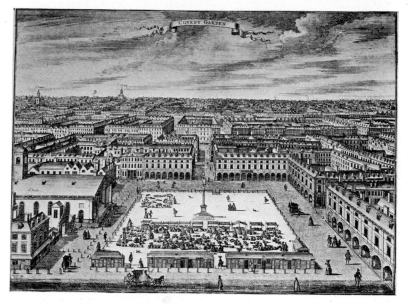

EIGHTEENTH CENTURY LONDON: A PROSPECT OF THE CITY AND A
VIEW OF COVENT GARDEN

France both unsuccessful and expensive. I had about me onely some bills of exchange upon a Jew called Medina for the sum of eight or nine [8] thousand French livres reckoning all. At my coming to London I found my damned Jew was broken; [9] I was without a penny, sick to death of a violent ague, a stranger, alone, helpless, in the midst of a city wherein I was known to no body; my Lord and my Lady Bolingbroke were in the country; I could not make bold to see our ambassadour [10] in so wretched a condition. I had never undergone such distress; but I am born to run through all the misfortunes of life." [11]

Could anything be more pathetic than this continued series of reverses? With touching humor Voltaire jokes of his bad fortune: " If the character of the hero of my poem is as well sustained as is that of my bad fortune, my poem will surely succeed better than I." [12] Indeed it seemed as if there were no limits to his bad luck. Six months before he had been fairly wealthy and much sought after in the dazzling society of the French capital; now he was literally a penniless exile, sick in body and in mind, without resources, almost without hope. It was the darkest moment in Voltaire's checkered existence; it was, however, but a forerunner of the dawn. " In these cir-

[8] Later on he mentions the sum as being twenty thousand livres.
[9] For this bankruptcy of Voltaire see: Lanson, *Revue latine*, 1908, p. 33, Voltaire et son banqueroutier juif en 1726; also: Foulet, *op. cit.*, p. 55, n.
[10] M. de Morville, the Secretary of State, had given Voltaire a letter to M. de Broglie, the French ambassador to England, which Voltaire subsequently presented.
[11] Foulet, *op. cit.*, Letter XXIX (not translated).
[12] Foulet, *op. cit.*, Letter XXIX.

cumstances," he writes, " my star, that among all its dire-
ful influences pours allways on me some kind refreshment,
sent to me an Englishman unknown to me, who forced me
to receive some money that I wanted.[13] Another London
citizen that I had seen but once at Paris, carried me to his
own house. . . ." [14]

The " other London citizen " here mentioned was
Everard Falkner, a rich English silk merchant who lived
in the quiet little village of Wandsworth, just outside of
London. During his stay in England, Falkner was one
of Voltaire's closest friends, and throughout his life Voltaire cherished the kindest regards for the man whose
home he had made his own during these trying years. In
1732 he dedicated *Zaïre* to Falkner in terms that aston-
ished the French, who could not conceive of a merchant
who was also a gentleman and a patron of letters. For
years they kept up an irregular correspondence, and in
1774, when two of Falkner's sons visited the patriarch at
Ferney, they received the most cordial reception. Taking
each by the hand Voltaire exclaimed, " Mon Dieu, que je
me trouve heureux de me voir entre deux Falkners."

Of Falkner himself we know little except that in 1735
he became English ambassador at Constantinople; later
he was confidential secretary to the Duke of Cumberland
for a number of years; and towards the end of the reign
of George II he became one of the Postmasters-General.
He died in 1758. We know even less of the personality,

[13] In the preface to an edition of his works published in London in
1746, Voltaire claims that this " English gentleman " was the king. This
claim is rather poorly substantiated, however, as M. Foulet points out:
op. cit., p. 58, n.

[14] Foulet, *op. cit.*, Letter XXIX (not translated).

of Falkner than we do of his career. Almost the only definite information we have on the subject comes from part of one of his letters which Voltaire quotes in his *Remarks on Pascal*, but this touch is charming enough to assure us that Voltaire's enthusiasm was not misplaced. " I am," writes Falkner, " just as you left me, neither merrier nor sadder, nor richer nor poorer; enjoying perfect health, having everything that renders life agreeable, without love, without avarice, without ambition, and without envy; and so long as all that lasts I shall call myself a very happy man."

After the trials of London, it must have been with a sigh of relief that Voltaire settled down in the restful atmosphere at Wandsworth. His previous study had worked off the roughest edges in his struggle with English, and he was now ready to attempt the mastery of its subtler points. He spent much time reading, and still more in conversation and argument. As an exercise he set himself the task of translating into English the Latin *Epistle* of Robert Barclay, the Quaker. He made occasional quick trips to London, where he probably saw Bolingbroke and others of that circle, but he was always glad to get back to his " obscure and charming life . . . quite given over to the pleasures of friendship and indolence," — " indolence " meaning to Voltaire freedom from social duties and time for reading.

By the end of October he seems to have acquired not only a fluent use of English, but also the English point of view. Writing to his friend Thieriot he says, " . . . all that is king, or belongs to a king, frights my republican philosophy. I won't drink the least drop of slavery in the land of liberty." " I fear, I hope nothing from *your* country. All that I wish for is to see you one day in London." [15] The comparison between England and France favored the former. Allowing for his characteristic dramatic exaggeration, Voltaire seems to be profoundly moved by his new associations.

The letter quoted above also leads us to suppose that at this time Voltaire was becoming acquainted with several English writers. The following passage sounds strangely like a Voltairian transcription of Shakespeare: " Life is but full of starts of folly and of fancied and true miseries. Death awakens us from this painful dream, and gives us either a better existence, or no existence at all! " And a passage upon Pope shows a remarkable choice of words for a person who has studied the language for little more than six months. " For my part," writes Voltaire, " I look upon his [Pope's] poem called the *Essay upon Criticism* as superior to the *Art of Poetry* of Horace; and his *Rape of the Lock, la boucle de cheveux* (that is a comical one), is in my opinion above the *Lutrin* of Despréaux; I never saw so amiable an imagination, so gentle graces, so great variety, so much wit, and so refined knowledge of the world as in this little performance." [16]

Barclay, Shakespeare, and Pope, however, were by no means the boundaries of Voltaire's reading. His investigation took him into almost every field. So much of our evidence about his life in England is necessarily circumstantial that we are very fortunate to have direct data on the scope of his interests during this period. A private

[15] Foulet, *op. cit.*, p. 61. (The italics are mine.)
[16] Foulet, *op. cit.*, p. 54.

note-book which he kept at this time gives us an intimate glimpse at his varied thoughts and interests. For the most part this note-book is in the form of short terse maxims, and of longer stories and anecdotes, often humorous, but always with a definite instructive point; sometimes he makes sweeping generalities, at other times he records particular incidents. The amount of space which he devotes to the differences between religions, and to the contradictions in various creeds, shows that comparative religion held great interest for him; a number of notes and anecdotes show that he was carefully studying the history of the country; while throughout the note-book there are fresh, clear impressions of contemporary England. There is neither consecutiveness nor the slightest order in the notes. Apparently they were quickly jotted down as a thought struck him. As these notes are an ignored portion of the literary work of Voltaire, it might be interesting to quote from them at length. The English, of course, is as Voltaire hastily jotted it down.

Starting off with religion Voltaire observes, " England is the meeting of all religions, as the royal exchange is the ' rendez-vous ' of all foreigners." Then turning his attention to the Quakers he makes the keen remark, " It seems that one does deal in England with the quakers as with the peers of the realm, which give their verdict upon their honour, not upon their oath." Contrasting England with France he says, " We arrive at the same work by different ways; a chartusian friar kneels and prostrates himself all along before me, a quaker speaks to me always covered, both do so to follow the Gospel in the most rigorous sense."

His tendencies toward deism are clearly shown in a number of remarks upon religion. " Ignorant supported by more ignorant men. Dunces are the founders of all religions; men of wit founders of all heresies; men of understanding laugh at both." And, " For to get some authority over others one must make oneself as unlike them as one can. 'Tis a sure way of dazzling the eyes of the crowd. So the priest appears in long gown, etc."

A weapon of which Voltaire was often to avail himself in the future, the use of historical criticism in matters of religion, is found here for the first time. " Jewish religion is the mother of Christianity, the grandmother of mohametism." " When I see Christians cursing Jews, methinks I see children beating their fathers." " One greatest error among Christians is about the holy ghost. Formerly when a man was made a lawyer in Jerusalem, he was [made] so by these words ' receive the holy ghost.' Now one does make use of the same words in making a priest." " 'Tis mere fancy to believe the character of a priest is indelible. A layman is made a clergyman only by designation; 'tis an office which can be revoked, and which was revoked effectually in the old ages of Christianity, when a priest wasted church and function." His familiarity with the procedure of the Quakers, with their lack of a definite preacher, may be seen in the following remark: " *Go and teach all nations.* This was said to all Christians before the distinction of clergy and layty."

His reading and investigation in the field of history proper range all the way from Caesar down to his own time. It is interesting to observe the variety of his records. " Three plagues in London under Elizabeth, Charles the

First, and Charles the Second." " Plutark tells us in Caesar's life he numbered the citizens in Rome and their number amounted to no more than an hundred and twenty thousand, which was but of three hundred and forty thousand [sic] before the civil wars. How that thinness of people may be reconciled with the prodigious populousness mentioned by other authors, 'tis hard to know: they talk of four millions in Augustus' time." " Cromwell built nothing. There is no monument remaining of him. His body together with those of Ireton and Bradshaw were taken out of their coffins at Westminster, and drawn upon hurdles to Tyburn where they were hanged by the neck for some hours, their heads chopt off afterwards and perched on Westminsterhall, 30 January 1661, a year after the restoration." " The same army that cut off Charles the first and Lawd [sic] was ready to make an arbitrary king of Charles 2 and a pope of the arch of Cant. . . ."

The care with which Voltaire did his historical research is illustrated by the astute accuracy of the following note on Cromwell: " They say Cromwell was nothing less than an enthusiast; he was so far from being a fanatic that he rul'd all who were so. He had a quick-sighted sagacity, a firm understanding and irresistible eloquence, a courage above all mankind, a profound knowledge of the world. He did not aim at first at the supreme power, but he was carried by degrees to the throne, making always the best use of the best circumstances. His humour was severe, but sometimes he indulged privately in some mirth with his private friends." He goes on to give an anecdote about a drinking bout of Cromwell, Milton, and Waller.

[101]

The most interesting things in this note-book, however, are Voltaire's comments on the English. In a few words he paints the English portrait, contrasting it very favorably with that of the French: " The English is full of thoughts, French all in miens, compliments, sweet words, and curious of engaging outside, overflowing in words, obsequious with pride, and very much self concern'd under the appearance of a pleasant modesty. The English is sparing of words, openly proud and unconcerned; he gives the most quick birth as he can to his thoughts, for fear of losing his time. English tongue, barren and barbarous in its origin, is now plentiful and sweet, like a garden full of exotik plants." In one incisive simile Voltaire sums up much that was most significant in eighteenth century English politics: " A king in England is a necessary thing to preserve the spirit of liberty, as a post to a fencer to exert himself." " In England everybody is publik spirited. In France everybody is concern'd in his own interest only." It is quite instructive to see this Frenchman, but a few months in the country, writing in such a tone about the England which but a few years before had been universally scorned by all his countrymen.

A comparison of Bolingbroke and Pope shows that already Voltaire knew them well enough to pick out their essential differences. " I think oft of Mr. B. and Mr. P. These are both virtuous and learned, of equal wit and understanding, but quite contrary in their ways. P. loves retirement and silence, virtuous and learned for himself. B. more communicative, diffuses everywhere his virtue and his knowledge. P. is a dark lanthorn: tho it is illuminated within, it affords no manner of light, or advantage to such as stood by it: the other is an ordinary lamp which consumes and wastes itself for the benefit of every passenger."

The scattered disorder of this note-book doubtless gives us a fair idea of Voltaire's life at Wandsworth. By means of conversation and of books he was picking up a thousand odd ends of information. An investigation as scattered as was his could not be logically followed out in the short time he had at his disposal, and Voltaire made little attempt to be logical. In the same breath he would dash from a statement of conditions in Lapland, to a piece of gossip about the Pope, and then to some extemporaneous verses of the Earl of Rochester. He would study with the greatest care the character of Cromwell and the history of Magna Charta. No piece of information was too minute for him to jot down, no subject too comprehensive for his investigation. During his stay in Wandsworth he was preparing an historical background for his future personal examination of England.[17]

In his search for knowledge and enlightenment Voltaire used his love for argument to great advantage. He would challenge to debate those who believed strongly in a certain point, bringing up every doubt that was in his mind. Later, among people of an opposite belief, turning about he would take up the case of those whom he had just opposed, forcing his adversaries to combat the arguments he himself had just heard. Thus, having seen both sides of the argument quite clearly, he was ready to make up his own mind.

[17] *The English Review*, February, 1914, pp. 313 ff., for this note-book.

In this connection there is an interesting anecdote, quite well authenticated,[18] which throws light on Voltaire's methods at this time. The story is related by a certain Edward Higginson, a Quaker, and was published in the *Hampstead Annual* for 1903. As it is typical of Voltaire, it might be interesting to quote it at length.

"Some time in the year 1724 [19] François Voltaire boarded a while with a scarlet dyer nigh the Friends' School at Halffarthing in the parish of Wandsworth, kept then by John Huweidt, with whom I had served about half my time. Voltaire desired to be improved in the English tongue; and in discourse with the master chanced to fall upon the subject of water-baptism which was treated between them, till, for want of understanding each other, they were so set they could proceed no further; when Voltaire inquired whether he had never an usher who understood Latin. There was one; but as he was not of our profession, my master thought him not suitable therefore sent for me into the parlour, and Voltaire rehearsed the conference, desiring, if he had missed, my master would put him right — but he had not. Then he began with me: and as they had been engaged for some time, there was less for me to advance. I then mentioned Paul's assertion in the 17th ver. I ch. I Cor. (For Christ sent me not to baptise, but to preach the Gospel), which seemed so strange, that in a violent passion, he said, I lied — which I put up patiently, till he, becoming cooler, desired to know why I would impose upon a stranger.

---

[18] See: Lanson's *Lettres Philosophiques*, Vol. I, pp. 19–22.
[19] This date is obviously a slip of memory. It is probably 1727. (*Cf.* Foulet, *op. cit.*, p. 93, n. 2.)

I said I had not imposed at all, but justly repeated the Apostle's words as they stood in our Bible. He replied, our Bible was falsely translated, and done by heretics. I desired to know whether he would be set down by Beza or Castalio. He styled them also heretics; I answered, I did presume he did not conceive that Paul's own hand-writing was extant: he replied he did not. I then inquired what he *would* be set down by: would he by the Greek? To this he assented, and thereon I fetched my Greek Testament, of Mathaire's edition in twelves, and referred him thereto: at the sight of which he was as much surprised as he was before enraged, desiring to know what our English clergy would object to this text. I said their general reply was, that Paul meant " not principally, or chiefly " : Voltaire observed, they, might in the same way elude all the rest of the book.

" Some short time after, Voltaire being at the Earl Temple's seat in Fulham, with Pope, and others such, in their conversation fell upon the subject of water-baptism — Voltaire assuming the part of the Quaker — and at length he came to mention that assertion of Paul. They questioned him there being any such assertion in all his writings; on which was a large wager laid as near as I remember of £500; and Voltaire not retaining where it was, had one of the Earl's horses, and came over the ferry from Fulham to Putney, and rode to Half-farthing; and alighting in the yard, desired our man to lead his horse about, being warm. Coming to my master, he asked for his little usher as he called me. When I came, he desired me to give him in writing the place where Paul said, *he was not sent to baptise.* — Which presently I did. Then

[105]

courteously taking his leave, he mounted and rode back
— and, of course, won his wager! "

Higginson goes on to say that Voltaire often read aloud
to him, usually from the *Spectator;* that he was translating Barclay's *Epistle* into English; and that he confessed to him that he was a deist.

Thus it was that Voltaire passed the summer and
autumn at Wandsworth. Long, quiet hours of conversation with his delightful host put him in touch with events
in contemporary England. Falkner was informed about
literature, commerce, and politics, and Voltaire made full
use of his friend's knowledge. Falkner's library supplied
him with the necessary historical and literary background.
In his excursions to the surrounding country he became
acquainted with the different points of view of Englishmen, and, above all, he got practice in speaking English.
At last he was ready to venture into London society.

Early in November we find Voltaire established in
London at Bolingbroke's house in Pall Mall. Among the
various people he met in England — and before he returned to France there was scarcely a person of any importance whom he had not at least met — the names of
three men stand out above all others as having had the
greatest influence upon him. Pope, Swift, and Bolingbroke
were constantly together during this period, and very
often Voltaire was to be found with one or another of
them. He was probably influenced more by what he heard
these men discuss, and by what he discussed with them,
than he was by all the books he read throughout his stay
in England. It was during this period — the winter and
spring of 1726–1727 — that he got to know them best.

Throughout the winter Pope divided his time between his house at Twickenham, just outside of the city, and London. In London he was usually to be found at Bolingbroke's, where, of course, Voltaire saw a great deal of him, and they soon became good friends. Each admired greatly the work of the other, and their relations seem to have been most cordial, despite certain rumors to the contrary which sprang up in after years. Swift had been in England during the summer of 1726, putting the finishing touches on *Gulliver's Travels,* which came out with the greatest success in the following October, but he had returned to Dublin before Voltaire's arrival in London. In April, 1727, he was again in London, and Voltaire at last had the chance to make his acquaintance. In June, Swift contemplated a short visit to Paris, and Voltaire at once gave the distinguished Englishman letters to many, of his friends. The death of George I, however, caused Swift to give up the trip.

Bolingbroke, who had been back from exile but a short time, was without political power. He had not been allowed to resume his place in the House of Lords, and at present he spent his time at the so-called " farm " at Dawley, where he painted rakes and pitchforks on the walls and gently mimicked the idyllic rustic life of Horace, as well as at his London house, where he indulged his unquenchable passion for politics. Voltaire was constantly with him in both of his residences. With the complete discredit which fell upon the Tories after the Pretender's unsuccessful attempt upon the throne in 1715, they had practically ceased to exist as a party of opposition. The only protests to be raised against Walpole's policies were the bitter polemics of the little group of writers centred about Bolingbroke. It was as a member of this group that Voltaire had his first taste of London life.

But Voltaire, bent upon seeing all sides of English life, was not content to find his friends merely among the opposition. Before quitting France he had taken the precaution to procure letters to men upon the other side of the political fence. De Morville, the Secretary of State for Foreign Affairs, had asked Horace Walpole, the English ambassador in France, to introduce Voltaire, and the latter had obligingly written the Duke of Newcastle and Bubb Dodington in the poet's favor. Dodington, who today enjoys a very malodorous reputation as a result of his various political treacheries and personal excesses, was still in high favor. He had not yet abandoned Walpole's camp, and at his country seat at Eastbury, Dorsetshire, was a liberal, if somewhat undiscriminating, patron of the arts. Through these men Voltaire became acquainted with different members of the court party, both nobles and politicians, and included the Prime Minister, Robert Walpole, among his friends.

Voltaire's life throughout most of the succeeding year is in vivid contrast to the quiet retirement of Wandsworth. With characteristic energy he plunged whole-heartedly into the social whirl of Pall Mall. Within a short time he had been received in most of the " salons " and meeting places of the fashionable world and men of letters. Apparently no door was closed to him; he was welcome everywhere.

A list of the places Voltaire visited during the years 1727–28 reads almost like an extract from a *Social Regis-*

Henry St John
Late Lord Viscount Bolingbroke

T. Murray pinxit

HENRY ST. JOHN, LORD VISCOUNT BOLINGBROKE

ter. Besides spending much time with Bolingbroke and Falkner, he spent three months at Peterborough's country seat at Parson's Green; he visited Walpole, indifferent to literature, but Prime Minister, and courted by Voltaire for his influence; Temple, the first Viscount of Palmerston, and one of Walpole's strongest supporters; Pultney, Count of Bath, and one of the organizers of the *Craftsman*; Chesterfield he saw before his embassy to the Hague (23 April, 1728); and Lord Hervey before his trip to Italy in 1728; Henry Fox; the Duchess of Queensbury, the protectress of the poet Gay; Dodington at Eastbury. He visited the Duchess of Marlborough at Blenheim, and doubtless saw Oxford on this same trip; he was very well received by Lord Bathhurst; Mrs. Howard (later the Countess of Suffolk) and Mrs. Clayton (better known as Lady Sundon) were among his friends; and the King and Queen themselves seem to have been well disposed toward him. Among men of letters his acquaintance seems to have been almost as wide. Besides Pope, Swift, and Bolingbroke, he knew the playwright Congreve, the poets Young and Thomson; Gay showed him the immortal *Beggar's Opera* before its appearance on the stage; he saw Pemberton's *A View of Isaac Newton's Life* before its publication in 1728; Dr. Clarke, the most accomplished of all Newton's disciples, was his guide in philosophical studies; he knew Mrs. Conduit, Newton's niece, and from her got the famous story of the falling apple which he preserved for future generations; Berkeley was among his friends, and so also Sir Hans Sloane, then president of the Royal Society (to membership in which Voltaire was afterwards elected), and Colley Cibber, who was at this time connected with the Drury Lane Theatre, and later became Poet laureate. The list is by no means complete, but it gives some idea of the extent of Voltaire's acquaintance.[20]

But, as usual, Voltaire refused to allow social obligations and attentions to monopolize all of his time. At Wandsworth he had become interested in the Quakers, and upon his arrival in London he continued his investigations of this sect, whose beliefs seemed so extraordinary to a Frenchman brought up on the strict formality of Catholicism. He took the trouble of looking up Andrew Pitt, one of the most prominent Quakers in England, and was charmed by his honest sincerity. In the *Lettres Philosophiques* Voltaire describes Pitt as " one of the most eminent Quakers in England, who, having traded thirty years, had the wisdom to prescribe limits to his fortune and desires, and settled in a little solitude at Hampstead." Voltaire took up with Pitt all the questions about Quakerism which his experience at Wandsworth had left unanswered, and thoroughly acquainted himself with all matters pertaining to their history, beliefs, and customs. It seems that he kept up his intercourse with Pitt throughout his stay in England.[21] The substance of his conversations with Pitt he has embodied in the article on Quakers in the *Dictionnaire Philosophique*, and in the first four of the *Lettres Philosophiques*. He was impressed by many of

[20] Baldensperger, *La chronologie du séjour de Voltaire en Angleterre; Archiv für das Studium der Neueren Sprachen und Literaturen*, 1913.

[21] Leonard Howard in his *Collection of Letters*, p. 604, prints a very keen letter supposedly written by Voltaire to Pitt, on Berkeley's *Alciphron*. Unfortunately the authenticity of this letter cannot be established. Collins quotes from it, *op. cit.*, p. 60.

the Quaker objections to the prevalent formality in religion, but the silent " waiting for inspiration " of a Quaker meeting was too much for him.

From the Quakers his attention turned to the various other sects, and in turn he examined the Church of England, the Presbyterians, the Unitarians, etc., summing up the religious situation in England with the delightful paradox, " If there were but one religion, there would be its despotism to fear; if there were two, they would cut each other's throats; but there are thirty, and they live in peace, happy."

Falkner was able to show Voltaire yet another important side of English life. He introduced him to the world of business and commerce, and impressed upon him their widespread influence and importance in the life of a community. Voltaire was probably thinking of his English friend when, in the letter on Commerce in the *Lettres Philosophiques,* he compares the usefulness of the powdered French lord who knows the exact hour when the king arises and retires, and the merchant " who enriches his country, who from his office gives orders in India and Egypt, and contributes to the happiness of the world." To a Frenchman accustomed to a social order which frowned forbiddingly on anything connected with business, this was a useful contrast to have emphasized.

Falkner's brother-in-law, P. Delme, could open yet another aspect of society to the traveller. Delme, who was very rich, was one of the most important dignitaries in London. He was intimately connected with the civic government, had been Lord Mayor in 1723–24, and was able

to show Voltaire at first hand the working of the munici-
pal government.

The theatre too had an important place in Voltaire's
life. With his knowledge of spoken English still none
too great, he took advantage of this chance to improve it.
He had obtained an introduction to Colley Cibber, who
gave him seats at the Drury Lane theatre. He was often
to be seen at the plays, following the action closely with
a printed copy of the play with which Cibber would pro-
vide him.[22] It is probable that at this time he gathered
most of the material for his future comparisons of the
English and the French stage. Among the plays which he
is likely to have seen are Addison's *Cato*, several of Shakespeare's plays including *Hamlet* and *Julius Caesar*,
Racine's *Andromaque*, Vanbrugh's *Provoked Wife*, Cibber's *Careless Husband*, Shadwell's *Don Juan*, Congreve's *Plain Dealer*, and Wycherly's *Country Wife*.[23]

By the beginning of 1728 Voltaire's acceptance by English society was given a fitting climax by his presentation
at court. In the *Daily Journal* [24] we find the following
record: " Last week M. Voltaire, the famous French poet,
who was banished from France, was introduced to his
majesty, who received him very graciously. They say he
has received notice from France not to print his Poems
of the League; a prosecution still pending against him,
by the Cardinal de Bissy, on account of the praises bestowed in that book on Queen Elizabeth's behavior in

[22] Chetwood, *History of the Stage*, p. 46.

[23] For other plays seen by Voltaire see Lanson's edition of the *Lettres
Philosophiques*, the list at the end of Letter XVIII. Also Lounsbury,
Voltaire and Shakespeare, p. 65.

[24] *The Daily Journal* (London), 27 January, 1727.

matters of Religion, and a great many strokes against the abuse of popery and against persecution in matters of faith."

London had become quite a different place for Voltaire since his unfortunate introduction to it in August, 1726. From being, "alone, helpless, in the midst of a city wherein I was known to nobody," he had risen to a position of social eminence in the English capital not far below the place he had occupied in his own Paris, before the Rohan incident. The rise in his fortunes in England had been almost as sudden, if not quite as unexpected, as had been his fall in France.

CHAPTER SEVEN
ENGLAND BUYS A POEM

CHAPTER SEVEN

ENGLAND BUYS A POEM

VOLTAIRE'S spontaneous acceptance by English society, pleasing as it was to his personal vanity, was still more welcome from a practical point of view. At last he had built up a stable foundation for the work which was the principal reason for his trip to England. Throughout the various incidents of his visit he had never lost sight of the *Henriade*. Writing to Thieriot in the autumn of 1726 he said: " I had a mind at first to print our poor Henry [the *Henriade*] at my own expense in London, but the loss of my money is a sad stop to my design. I question if I shall try the way of subscriptions by the favour of the court. I am weary of courts, my dear Thieriot. . . ." [1] But it was never very difficult for Voltaire to rid himself of his prejudices against kings and courts — they were ever among his pet weaknesses. What influenced him far more was the fact that until he became well known in England there was little chance that the venture would be a financial success, and financial success is one of the key-notes of Voltaire's career. Consequently, when Voltaire emerged from his retirement at Wandsworth into the light gaiety of Pall Mall he kept constantly before him the idea of advancing the *Henriade*. Wherever he went, he kept the name of his favorite poem ever in the ears and minds of those whom he met. He was always " M. de

[1] Foulet, *op. cit.*, p. 61.

Voltaire, the author of the *Henriade.*" Whenever he could get his name into the papers, he made sure that coupled with it was the name of his poem. There is not a single press notice about him in the English papers from the beginning of his visit to the end which does not bring in the *Henriade* whenever Voltaire is mentioned. Voltaire was one of the early masters in the art of advertising; he fully realized the value of keeping a name always before the public.

Basing his hopes upon the warmth of his personal reception, it seemed to Voltaire early in 1727 that he might with safety start to solicit subscribers for the great edition of his epic. For a while his prospects were bright. Many of his friends used their influence in favor of the work. The Prime Minister, Robert Walpole, found time to solicit subscribers; he even used his influence with members of the diplomatic corps.[2] Nevertheless, the number of subscriptions received was not sufficient to warrant the publication of the work. Hurt by this failure, and impatient to get the edition printed, Voltaire seems to have contemplated returning to France to survey conditions there. Either at the end of March, or in the first part of April, he applied for permission to return to Paris. After some correspondence, his request was granted, on the twenty-ninth of June. But by this time the outlook in

[2] On the third of March, 1727, M. de Broglie, the French ambassador in London, wrote M. de Morville, the French Secretary of State, to find out the attitude of his government toward this work. " Il [Voltaire] me solicite," writes de Broglie, " de lui procurer des souscrivants, et M. de Walpole s'employe de son côté tout de son mieux pour tâcher de lui en faire avoir le plus grand nombre qu'il sera possible. . . ." Jusserand, *English Essays from a French Pen*, p. 214.

England was brightening, and Voltaire decided to prolong his stay.

It might be well to note in passing the change in Voltaire's mental attitude shown by his refusal to make use of this permission to return to Paris. Up to this point his stay in England really amounted to exile. Now he had official permission to return. Although the order was temporary, being limited to three months,[3] it was tacitly understood that this was a probationary period. Had he behaved to the satisfaction of the authorities during these first three months the permit would have been made permanent. But Voltaire of his own free will decided to remain in England. His admiration for the English, and for their political system, which allowed such personal liberty and such freedom of expression, was rapidly growing. A comparison of the advantages of the two countries found much on the English side.

In his activities in publishing the *Henriade* we have a most characteristic example of Voltaire's tireless energy and resource. Since the work had first been published clandestinely in 1723, he had cherished the idea of bringing out this de Luxe edition, with full text and illustrations, an edition that would be worthy of the poem which he hoped would become the immortal epic of France. A number of people had subscribed to the proposed edition, some years before Voltaire went to England, but the strictness of the censorship had always made publication

[3] This permission was good for three months, not for nine, as is stated by Collins (p. 54). The manuscript of the letter of Maurepas to Voltaire conveying the permission is in the Archives Nationales (Paris) (o¹ 374 f° 288). The entire letter is reprinted by Foulet, *op. cit.*, Letter XL.

impossible. When he reached England he hoped, as we have seen, to print the long-awaited edition there at his own expense, and then smuggle it into France. When the loss of his money forced him to abandon this design, a still better one came to him. Instead of risking his own capital, and taking the chance of having the entire edition confiscated as he tried to get it into France, why not arouse the interest of the English in the work to a point where he could finance the edition from their subscriptions? When the list of subscribers fell short of the number requisite for financial success, he realized that what was needed was more publicity, and he set to work accordingly.

During the summer and fall of 1727 much of his time was spent in retirement near Wandsworth in the preparation of a masterpiece of advertising, and one of the most extraordinary works in literary history. To arouse interest in his poem, he determined to prepare two essays, written in English, one upon the *Civil Wars of France,* the subject of the *Henriade,* the other an essay on *Epic Poetry* from Homer to Milton. The English might not be interested in a long epic poem, written in a foreign language about foreign conditions and people; they would be most interested in two essays written in their own language by a foreigner who had studied the language only a little over a year.

The essay on epic poetry interested him intensely. Comparative literature, the observation of the " different genius of each nation," was at this time little studied, and less understood. Voltaire had long desired to study this interesting topic; the necessities of the *Henriade* now gave him an opportunity to do so. Starting with Homer and

aft Plates, made
... in the

fived here from ...

I. S. 'On the
ie Eagle Galley,
ell, from New-
a Sailor, ship-
ndland, was in
over-board, and
bility it will not
paniards declare
e making great
is; their Gene-
ficers are arriv'd

Since the 31ft
e Silphidia, John
the Margaret,
1; the Neptune,
nburgh; and the
ell, from Cork.
iiled the Jupiter,
for China; the
lon Diego Ari-
the Friendship,
the Edward and
both for San Lu-
amuel, William
the Knight Gal-
or the Streights.
l, 9 French, 2
rgher. ———
nd Dutch Mer-
uch Hints from
as have given
it them upon ta-

ters from St. Chriftopher s, which lay,
They had there an Account that the Fair
... Gallafpy, bound from
... land with Negroes, had
... e Coaft of Guiney; by
... to Briftol, whofe Crew
lately ... rates.

The Rebecca of Briftol, Capt. Rofe,
bound from New-England, to Bilboa,
was lately loft within the Bar of Bilboa
and part of her Crew were drowned.

Laft Week M. Voltaire, the famous
French Poet, who was banifh'd from
France, was introduc'd to his Majefty,
who received him very gracioufly. They
fay he has received Notice from France,
not to print his Poems of the League; a
Profecution ftill depending againft him,
by the Cardinal de Biffy, on the Account
of the Praifes beftow'd in that Book, on
Queen Elizabeth's Behaviour in Matters
of Religion, and a great many Strokes
againft the Abufe of Popery, and againft
Perfecution in Matters of Faith.

'Tis faid, that the French Court is
about to undertake a fecret Expedition in
favour of the Allies of Hanover

One hundred and Twenty able-bodied
Men, that had inlifted themfelves as Re-
cruits for the Garrifons of Gibraltar and
Port-Mahon, were on Tuefday laft put on
Ship-board from the Savoy.

Mr. Serjeant Chefhire, is made his
Majefty's Premier Serjeant at Law, in the
Room of the now Lord Chief Baron
Pengelly.

Laft Night the Earl of Radnor arrived
at St. James's from his Travels.

As did alfo Sir Charles Cornwallis
Lloyd, Bart, from his Seat in Cardigan-
fhire, to be married to Mifs Brydges.

Saturday laft, William Bethel, of the

PAGE OF CONTEMPORARY NEWSPAPER SHOWING VOLTAIRE'S
PUBLICITY METHODS

Virgil, he discussed in turn Italian, Spanish, Portuguese, and English epics, analyzing them with his usual combination of keen perception and hurried superficiality; and always, by his inimitable turning of phrases and thoughts, calling attention to the multiple interests and superiorities of the forthcoming *Henriade*. In all that concerned England he was mindful of the audience for which he was writing. The passage on Milton contains a good deal of rather exaggerated praise, which does not tally exactly with what we know of Voltaire's personal opinion of the English poet. Addison he calls, " The best Critic as well as the best Writer of his age "; [4] and Pope's translation of Homer is praised to the skies. With deft flattery he called attention to the fact that while France possessed no epic at all, England boasted a model of that art. Interested as he really was in the subject he was treating, he still allowed no consideration to lessen the advertising value of the essay.

The publication of such a work required a great amount of preparation, and Voltaire devoted most of the summer and autumn of 1727 to the task. During this period he paid occasional visits to various friends at their country seats, but most of the time he was to be found in his quiet retreat near Wandsworth, working away at this new enterprise. When we consider the content of the essay, and the fact that Voltaire was writing in a foreign language, it is not hard to imagine that the work took even this genius of rapid accomplishment a good deal of time to complete. He claims to have made original discoveries concerning the life of Milton; at least he did make an

<hr/>

[4] White, *Voltaire's Essay on Epic Poetry*, p. 134.

exhaustive and sympathetic study of *Paradise Lost*. He was familiar with Virgil and Tasso, and to some extent with Lucan and Homer, but the *Araucana* of Alonzo of Ercilla, and the *Lusiad* of Camoens, were fields which he had to explore for the first time. Above all, the attempt to understand and to appreciate the individuality of different nations was a novel idea, and one which required astute observation and research.

The Essay upon the Civil Wars in France is an historical sketch of France between the accession of Francis II and Henry IV's entrance into Paris, a theme with which Voltaire was intimately acquainted, and which probably caused him less trouble than did the other subject. The two essays are not in the stiff, strained style which might be expected of a foreigner, but, on the contrary, the language is smooth and plastic, not far below Voltaire's peerless style in his own language. Indeed, Churton Collins [5] has said: "If Voltaire was able after a few months' residence in London to produce such prose as this, it is not too much to say that he might with time and practice have taken his place among our national classics."

Early in December the essays appeared in an octavo edition of one hundred and thirty pages. Their success was instantaneous, and within a few weeks a second edition was announced; by 1731 [6] the little book had been printed five times. [7] The essays were successful not only in a literary way, but also, as Voltaire had intended, as advertisement. The public at once recognized the real

[5] Churton Collins, *op. cit.*, p. 67.
[6] This date is approximate. *Cf.* White, *op. cit.*, p. 8.
[7] On the different editions of the *Essays* see: White, *op, cit.*, p. 8.

purpose of the work, and the greatest interest in the *Henriade* was stimulated. The following item which appeared in *The Present State of the Republic of Letters* gives an idea of the attitude of the public: " We also hope every day to see Mr. De Voltaire's *Henriade*. He has greatly raised the expectation of the curious, by a beautiful essay he has lately published upon the Civil Wars of France (which is the subject of his poem), and upon the epic poets from Homer down to Milton. As this gentleman seems to be thoroughly acquainted with all the best poets, both ancient and modern, and judges so well of their beauties and faults, we have reason to hope that the *Henriade* will be a finished performance; and as he writes with uncommon elegance and force in English, though he has been but eighteen months in this country, we expect to find in his poem all that beauty and strength of which his native language is capable." [8]

Coincident with the publication of the essays, Voltaire started the printing of the *Henriade*. At last public interest had been sufficiently aroused, and his beloved edition was on its way. The book was ready for distribution in January, 1728, but for two months it was held back, while a final advertising campaign was launched. The fact that Voltaire had been refused permission to print the poem in France because of its attitude toward the Church, was splendid capital. All opposition to Rome was welcome in England. Besides notices in the newspapers, and the general attention that was attracted by the essays, Voltaire's advertising campaign included personal

[8] *The Present State of the Republic of Letters*, January, 1728, Vol. I, p. 88.

letters to prospective subscribers. An example of his method of procedure, and especially of his accustomed use of flattery, is to be found in a letter which he wrote at this time to the Count of Oxford. " My Lord," writes Voltaire, " though I am a traveller unknown to yr Lordship, the name of Harlay has been for many centuries so glorious among us French, and the branch of yr house settled in France is so proud of the honour of being nearly related to yrs that you must forgive the liberty of this letter.

" I have written and printed here a book called the *Henriade* in which one Harlay of yr house acts the most noble part and such a one as you should be acquainted with. For my part, having been in some measure educated in the house of the late Achilles de Harlay, the oracle and first president of our Parliament, I should be wanting to my duty if I durst not trouble yr lordship about it and beg the favour of waiting upon you before the book comes out. . . ." [9] This letter does not seem to have borne fruit, for we do not find the name of the Count of Oxford on the list of subscribers.

This advertising campaign of Voltaire's would do justice to a highly trained specialist of our own time. It is interesting to find this eighteenth century poet using all the devices which we are accustomed to think of as particular to modern ingenuity. Even if we do not greatly admire his poetry today, at least Voltaire's business acumen should strike a responsive chord.

As a final means of acquiring good will for the book,

[9] Foulet, *op. cit.*, p. 114. This letter is published for the first time by M. Foulet.

Voltaire cancelled his former dedication to Louis XV, and substituted for it a very flattering eulogy of Caroline, the English Queen. " It is the fate of Henry the Fourth," wrote Voltaire, " to be protected by an English queen. He was assisted by that great Elizabeth who was in her age the glory of her sex. By whom can his memory be so well protected as by her who resembles so much Elizabeth in her personal virtues? . . . Our Descartes, who was the greatest philosopher in Europe before Sir Isaac Newton appeared, dedicated his *Principles* to the celebrated princess Palatine, Elizabeth, not, said he, because she was a princess, for true philosophers respect princes, and never flatter them, but because of all his readers she understood him the best, and loved truth the most. I beg leave, Madam (without comparing myself to Descartes), to dedicate the *Henriade* to Your Majesty, upon the like account, not only as the protectress of all arts and sciences, but as the best judge of them." [10]

When in March the book finally appeared Voltaire was amply repaid for the pains he had taken in promoting it. The subscription list was headed by the King and Queen, and included almost every distinguished person in the political, social, and literary world of the times. Several of his friends took a number of copies; Bolingbroke and Peterborough were each down for twenty copies, Chesterfield for ten. By the time the quarto edition appeared every copy had been taken. Within three weeks there was a cheaper octavo edition. Voltaire, writing to a French friend soon after, says: " Though the poem is written in a language not much admired here in regard

[10] *La Henriade de M. de Voltaire*, London, 1728, in 4°.

to poetry, yet three editions have been made in less than three weeks, which I assure you I attribute entirely to the lucky subject I have pitched upon, and not at all to the performance." [11] Voltaire might have remarked that the popularity of the subject in England was not entirely due to luck. The advertising campaign had done its work.

In connection with the printing of the cheaper editions, Voltaire is reported to have had a quarrel with one of his publishers. It seems more than likely, however, that this disagreement was merely arranged for advertising purposes.

It is difficult to estimate exactly the extent of the financial success of the book, but it is certain that Voltaire realized a good deal of money from it. Nicolardot [12] estimates the sum at ten thousand francs, which is the lowest possible figure; Collins [13] estimates the total sum, including a gift of five hundred pounds from the king, at two thousand pounds sterling, a figure which is scarcely exaggerated.

Whatever the exact amount, it was more than welcome to Voltaire, who had been in straitened circumstances for most of his stay in England. The struggle had been long and arduous, he had met with many set-backs, but the final result was in the grand style so dear to Voltaire's vanity.

[11] Foulet, *op. cit.*, p. 136.
[12] *Ménages et Finances de Voltaire*, p. 63.
[13] Collins, *op. cit.*, p. 78.

CHAPTER EIGHT
LAST MONTHS OF EXILE

CHAPTER EIGHT

LAST MONTHS OF EXILE

THERE are few periods of Voltaire's life about which we have less definite information than that from March to December, 1727. His correspondence, usually such a fertile source of information, is almost non-existent. There is a short, semi-official note to Maurepas about his proposed return to France; one letter to Thieriot dated the twenty-seventh of May; and a short note to Swift enclosing some letters of introduction for the English writer in France. Except for these letters we have no news of him until the publication of the two essays in English in the following December. Not only did Voltaire himself cease writing, but during this period he received little news from France — even his intimate friend Thieriot stopped writing.[1] The explanation of this apparent blank space in Voltaire's life is that at last he had settled down to literary work. He had gone back to Wandsworth, and again was living a life of retirement.

Voltaire's decision to quit the gayety of London after such a brief taste of it was not altogether uninfluenced. Living in London society was a very expensive pleasure.

[1] In the following April (1728) Voltaire wrote to Thieriot: "That I love you is very certain; that I have never received a letter from you these ten months, and that I should have received them, had you written any, is equally true." (Foulet, *op. cit.*, p. 134.) [Thieriot claimed that he had written a number of letters to Voltaire.]

Among other things the item of tips was considerable. At no house in London was this abuse more pronounced than at Lord Chesterfield's, and Voltaire, who dined there once, was so annoyed that on being asked to repeat his visit, he declined, adding sarcastically that his lordship's ordinary was too dear.[2]

A few months of this life had cut considerably into Voltaire's resources, which were already in a rather precarious state. We are ignorant of just what means Voltaire found to meet the expenses of this short entry into society, but by various expedients he was able to get along temporarily. In December, 1726, he received another financial setback. In that month the French government made heavy cuts in the payment of life annuities, ruining many and causing others, among them Voltaire, very great losses.[3] A final blow came with the loss of his pensions, which he was unable to collect owing to his absence.[4] So desperate had his financial condition become, that when Thieriot, early in 1727, wrote asking him to buy a num-

[2] John Taylor, *Memoirs*, Vol. I, p. 330. An account of these conditions is found in De Saussure's *Letters*, p. 194: "If you wish to pay your respects to a nobleman, and to visit him, you must give his porter money from time to time, else his master will never be at home to you. If you take a meal with a person of rank you must give every one of the five or six footmen a coin when leaving. They will be ranged in file in the hall, and the least you can give them is one shilling each, and should you fail to do this you will be treated insolently the next time. My Lord Southwell stopped me one day in the Park, and reproached me most amicably with having let some time pass before going to his house to have soup with him. 'In truth, my Lord,' I answered, 'I am not rich enough to take soup with you often.' His lordship understood my meaning and smiled." These incidents are quoted by Collins, p. 82.

[3] Foulet, *op. cit.*, p. 78, note 3.

[4] *Ibid.*, p. 79, note 1.

This View of the R. Hon.ble the Earl of CHESTERFIELD'S House, near Hyde Park, taken from ye Park Wall.
is Humbly Dedicated to his Lordship by his Lp.s Most Obedient Servant Ed. D. Eyre.

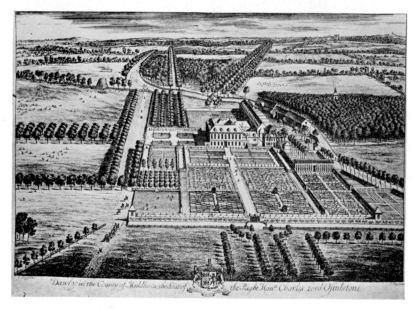

Draw.n in the County of Middlesex the Seat of the Right Hon.ble Charles Lord Ossulstone.

ENGLISH RESIDENCES ASSOCIATED WITH VOLTAIRE: CHESTERFIELD'S HOUSE
AND LORD BOLINGBROKE'S COUNTRY SEAT

ber of books, Voltaire was unable to do so. He wrote his
friend that if he could collect some of his debts in Paris
for him, he, Voltaire, would be glad to purchase the
books, but that he was unable to do so with the funds he
had on hand.[5]

Voltaire's health also influenced his decision to return
to Wandsworth. The English climate never agreed with
him, and his letters are full of complaints about it. When
he arrived in London he was " sick to death of a violent
ague," and illness was his constant companion. In a
letter to Dr. Towne written just before his return to
France he says: " I want a warmer climate for my health,
which grows worse and worse in England." [6] His first
letter upon his return to France gives a graphic description of his languishing in England: " To have a passing
fever, or the smallpox is nothing, but to be oppressed by
a feeling of faintness for whole years, to see all one's
relish for things destroyed, to have yet enough life to
want to enjoy it but too little strength to do so, to become
useless and unbearable to oneself, to die little by little,
that is what I have suffered, and what has been more
cruel than all my other trials." [7] The rich food and irregular hours of society life had been especially bad for
his fragile system, and during his stay in London he was
constantly under the care of a doctor.[8] It is one of the
ironies of fate that this man who so loved the glamour
and the contacts of society was endowed with a body that
was unable to stand the strain of such a life — yet it is
doubtless partly due to this very fact that he was able to

[5] *Ibid.*, p. 79.
[6] *Ibid.*, Letter LVI.
[7] *Ibid.*, Letter LXI, translated.
[8] *Ibid.*, Letter XXXII.

leave behind him such a monument of literary achievement.

Voltaire probably retired to Wandsworth some time in April, 1727. In May he wrote to Thieriot from his quiet retreat that he had been very ill, but was at last recovering. In ending the letter with a repentant note about his own over-indulgence in society, he transcribes an epigram of Martial,

" *Tomorrow I will live, the fool does say.*
Today's too late, the wise liv'd yesterday.

I am the fool, be the wise, and farewell." [9]

Voltaire was not sorry to have to go back to Wandsworth. He had now been in England almost a year, and had collected a mass of literary material of various sorts. He had constantly been gathering different items of information which were later included in the *Lettres Philosophiques*, the *Histoire de Charles XII*, the *Siècle de Louis XIV*, the *Dictionnaire Philosophique*, the *Essai sur la Poésie Epique*, etc. He was glad of the chance to work over this material. Moreover he had become interested in the stage in England, and had already conceived two plays which show the undoubted influence of Shakespeare and the English tradition — *César* and *Brutus*. He took this opportunity to work on these also. But, of course, the thing of most importance at the moment was the preparation of the *Essay on Epic Poetry*, and the *Essay on the Civil Wars of France*, and it was to these that Voltaire gave the greatest part of his attention. Throughout the summer and fall he was busily engaged in

[9] *Ibid.*, Letter XXXVII.

this literary work. The secluded country life agreed with him, and he was keenly interested in these new studies.

By November the two essays were finished and he returned to London to supervise their publication. His previous experience in the English capital had taught him a lesson, and he avoided the social life which, though so pleasing, had ended so unhappily. He now took up his residence in the studious Covent Garden quarter, and there we find him in December, when the essays were finally published, established at the White Peruke, within a short distance of the offices of various publishers. He was now engaged in the reading of proof and the other matters of routine entailed by the publication of two books.

This change of residence gave Voltaire a view of another side of English life. It was doubtless at this time that he frequented the Bedford Head tavern, the famous meeting place of men of letters, where legend has it that Voltaire was a frequent visitor. The Rainbow Coffee House, the rendezvous of the French refugees, is another tavern where Voltaire is supposed to have spent much time at this period. At the latter place he was in contact with men of his own race who were thoroughly acquainted with English conditions, and he was glad to compare with them impressions about the two countries. If his various necessities did force him to give up his former friends (he writes Swift in March that he has not seen Pope all winter),[10] they also gave him a chance to see something of the bohemian side of London life.

[10] *Ibid.*, p. 109.

With the publication of the *Henriade* there was no longer need for Voltaire to live near his publishers, and he moved again, this time settling in Billiter Square, a stone's throw from the Stock Exchange, and around the corner from his agents, Simon and Benezet. Bolingbroke had given up his town house,[11] and Voltaire still found it wiser to avoid the trials of society life. Two interesting anecdotes, which throw some light upon Voltaire's experience in England, belong to this period. The French were unpopular with the common people in England at this time, and Voltaire, who always looked unmistakably French, at times found himself in an uncomfortable position. Once when he was walking through the slums of London, he found himself surrounded by a hostile, jeering crowd who were debating what they should do with the "French dog." Soon they began hurling more substantial objects than epithets, and his position became dangerous. Voltaire's wit, however, was equal to the emergency. Boldly facing his assailants, he delivered an eloquent oration. "Brave Englishmen," he began, " am I not sufficiently unhappy in not having been born among you? " The rest of the speech has not been preserved, but its effect is said to have been instantaneous. From hostility the attitude of the crowd was changed to tolerance, then to enthusiasm, and they ended by carrying the Frenchman triumphantly back to his lodgings upon their shoulders.[12]

The other anecdote, which shows us one way in which Voltaire collected his impressions of England, we have

---

[11] *Ibid.*, p. 134, note 3.
[12] Longchamp et Wagnière, *Mémoires sur Voltaire*, Vol. 1, p. 45.

from Voltaire himself. "One day when I was in a boat on the Thames, one of my oarsmen, seeing I was a Frenchman, began in a proud way to boast to me about the liberty of his country and said to me, with an oath, that he would rather be a boatman on the Thames than Archbishop in France. Next day I happened to pass a prison, and I saw the very same man in it; there were irons on his feet, and through the bars he was holding out his hand to the passersby. I asked him if he still thought so poorly of Archbishops in France, and he recognized me. 'Ah! sir, what an abominable government ours is! I have been seized by main force to go and serve on one of the King's ships in Norway. I have been torn away from my wife and children, and, for fear that I should take flight, I have been thrown into prison, with irons on my feet, till the day I shall have to embark.'

"This man's misfortune, and such a crying injustice, sensibly affected me. A Frenchman who was with me confessed that he felt a malicious joy to see that the English, who are so loud in their reproaches of our servitude, were just as much slaves as ourselves. But I had a more humane feeling. I was distressed that there was not more liberty on the earth." [13]

With the coming of spring the atmosphere of London seemed less attractive, and Voltaire once more returned to Wandsworth, and busied himself with literary pursuits. He was still not satisfied with the form of the *Henriade,* and spent some time making alterations and corrections on it. The *Essay on Epic Poetry,* too, came in for its share of attention. The English edition of that

[13] Moland, *op. cit.,* Vol. XXII, p. 22.

work was, as Voltaire says, " but a sketch of a very serious work," which he was writing in French, " with all
the care, the liberty, and the impartiality I am capable
of." [14] At Wandsworth he completed this essay, which is
quite a different work from the English essay on the same
subject. He also worked on the *Lettres Philosophiques*.

Two other books, however, probably took up most of
his time during this period. When he returned to France,
Voltaire had practically completed his delightful biography, the *Histoire de Charles XII*, which he published
in 1731; and his tragedy *Brutus*, the first act of which
he wrote in English, was fully outlined.

The *Histoire de Charles XII* is an excellent example
of the way in which Voltaire turned his social friendships
to literary account. When he left France he had only a
general knowledge of the life of Charles XII. But in
England he came into contact with a man who was more
qualified than anyone in the world to supply data for such
a biography, Baron Frederic Ernest Fabrice. In 1710,
Fabrice had been sent on an embassy to Charles XII by
Prince Christian Augustus of Holstein. His pleasant ways
greatly charmed the Swedish king, who insisted that
Fabrice remain with him, and for some years he lived with
Charles at Bender, soon becoming one of his most intimate friends. The two were constant companions throughout this period, and it was due to Fabrice's enthusiasm that
the Swedish king became interested in the French writers,
Corneille, Racine, and Boileau. This close personal asso-
ciation with Charles gave Fabrice an excellent knowledge
of the character of the Swedish king. He was with Charles

[14] Foulet, *op. cit.*, Letter LIX.

at his disastrous meeting with the Turks, and at the last moment tried, unsuccessfully, to act as mediator between the two forces. Fabrice had also been a close friend of George I of England, and was in the carriage with him at Osnabrück at the time of his death. In August, 1727, he arrived in England, bringing with him the valuables which the English king wore at the time of his death. For some time after this he remained in England, living at Chesterfield's house in Saint James' Square, and mixing in the same society as did Voltaire.

Voltaire probably met Fabrice casually, and became interested in the subject of Charles XII through Fabrice's endless anecdotes and reminiscences of the great king. Struck by the possibilities of a biography, Voltaire immediately set to work to extract the necessary information from the Swedish nobleman. By diligent investigation he cleared up point after point in the life of Charles, mixing fact and anecdote in his inimitable way. Although dependent on Fabrice for the greater part of his material, Voltaire was not content to accept his unsupported statement. There were other people in England who could give information about the Swedish king, and they too were called upon to contribute their share. Jeffreys, who had been the English minister to Charles when Fabrice was with him at Bender, was invaluable in giving the impression the Swedish king made upon those who were less intimate with him than was Fabrice. The Duchess of Marlborough described in detail a famous interview which had taken place twenty years before between her husband and Charles at a moment when the allies were anxiously endeavoring to find out what part Sweden was likely to play in the coming war; and she doubtless supplied other valuable information. Bolingbroke was called upon for his contribution of anecdotes and impressions, as were various other persons who had been at Charles' court. Voltaire combed England for any material which might help him.

Thus was evolved this fascinating biography which has always been among the most popular of Voltaire's books. He made great use of friends and social acquaintances; an afternoon tea might supply a useful anecdote; a chat after dinner might clear up a troublesome point; a week-end house party might be the inspiration of an important chapter. It would seem that it was purely a matter of chance that the work was ever written. It *was* a matter of chance — chance, and Voltaire's genius for making instant use of any opportunity which presented itself.

Such literary work kept Voltaire busy at Wandsworth during the summer of 1728, but all the time he was debating in his mind what his future plans would be. Just as the *Henriade* was one of the most important influences in deciding Voltaire upon his trip to England, and in governing his conduct while he was there, so also it was influential in bringing him back to his native land. As soon as the *Henriade* had been published in London, the restless mind of Voltaire started at once to figure on the possibilities of bringing out a still better edition in his own country. He had written Thieriot to see if he would not supervise the publication of such a work, but his friend, either because of his great laziness, or through fear of royal prosecution, declined the responsibility, and suggested that Voltaire himself do it. Voltaire hesitated for a while, and finally decided that it might be well to return to his native land.

With the publication of the London edition of his epic poem in the spring of 1728, the main reason for Voltaire's presence in England disappeared, and the following months see him gradually lose interest in his adopted country. For the first time since the beginning of his exile he looks with longing eyes toward the gayety of Paris, unmindful of the superior liberty and freedom of England. Even the quiet solitude of Wandsworth, with its leisure for literary pursuits, loses some of its charm. This growing homesickness for the old Parisian haunts is shown by an outburst at the end of one of his letters to Thieriot. ". . . write me, I beseech you," pleads Voltaire, " oftener than I write you. I live in a retreat about which there is nothing to tell, while you are in Paris where every day you see new extravagances which might still please your poor friend, who is unhappy enough not to be able to enjoy them." [15] This is indeed a change of mind from the contented boast of two years before: " I fear, I hope nothing from your country." Plainly the spell of England had begun to break.

As his thoughts turned toward home, Voltaire once more recalled the conditions of his departure from Paris, and for the first time in over two years he alludes to Rohan. Writing in the middle of June to Thieriot about the proposed publication of the French *Essai sur la poésie épique* and of the *Henriade*, Voltaire says: " The printing of them both is a duty I must discharge before I think of other duties less suitable with the life of a man of letters,

[15] Foulet, *op. cit.*, p. 176 (translated).

but becoming a man of honour, and from which you may be sure I shall never depart as long as I breathe." The defiant tone of this passage would lead one to believe that Voltaire still desired revenge from Rohan, but it seems more than likely that this was merely an attempt to find whether Paris still remembered that humiliating event. Never again in the correspondence of this period does Voltaire mention Rohan, or that unpleasant affair. Apparently Thieriot wrote back that the whole thing had been forgotten in Paris, and Voltaire, realizing that nothing could be gained by re-opening the matter, was content to leave it as it was.

By the middle of June, Voltaire seems to have made up his mind to return to France. His plan was to go into hiding in some small place in the country until events were favorable for his entry into Paris. In a letter of the fourteenth of June he informs Thieriot of this project, but he carefully cautions him, " let nobody be acquainted with the secret of my being in France. I should be exceedingly glad, my dear Thieriot, of seeing you again, but I would see nobody else in the world." Another letter shows us that two months later Voltaire was still engaged in his literary work at Wandsworth. After this letter, in which he does not refer to his proposed return to France, we have no word from him until the following February, when he writes Thieriot that he is hiding in France, " upon the footing of an English traveller." [16] Sometime between August, 1728, and February, 1729, Voltaire returned to his native land. As a letter from Lord Peterborough to Towne which M. Foulet has accurately dated

[16] Foulet, *op. cit.*, p. 182.

November fourteenth, 1728, announces that Voltaire has already left England, it seems likely that the departure took place either in September or October of this year.[17] He had been in England approximately two years and three months.

[17] *Id.*, p. 270 ff.

CHAPTER NINE
HEARSAY AND SLANDER

CHAPTER NINE

HEARSAY AND SLANDER

SEVERAL malicious stories concerning Voltaire's stay in England sprang up after his return to France. One hesitates even to refute these stories for fear their repetition may keep them from the oblivion they deserve. The longer the time after Voltaire's departure from England, the more frequently were the stories repeated, and the more bitter became the attack. It is possible that the mere existence of these stories may lead some people to believe that there is a basis of fact for them. Before condemning Voltaire by such circumstantial evidence, one should remember two of his salient qualities. His wit was sharp, biting, and cruel; and, for the greater part of his life, he carried on a bitter attack upon certain established institutions, and especially upon the Church. Often Voltaire's wit offended sensitive people, leaving around him enemies eager for a chance to harm him. These contemporaries were quick to find a weapon of revenge in the slightest incident, and if a plausible excuse for attack were not to be found in the realm of fact, they drew upon their imaginations for calumnies. Often there was not the slightest authority for their statements. In his later life, Voltaire's attacks upon the Church increased his enemies a thousand fold, and all about him defenders of the established order and of morality lost no opportunity to defame his character. Just as Voltaire was violently intolerant in his attacks upon intolerance, so were these zealots unrestrictedly immoral in attacking this " apostle of immorality." As long as theirs was a righteous struggle, they had no scruples as to their weapons. The existence of such an origin of defamatory attacks must not, of course, tempt us to set aside all stories derogatory to Voltaire, but it must make us cautious in accepting anecdotes at face value.

Of the various stories which sprang up in England about Voltaire, those concerning his relations with Pope are the most persistent, and have been given more general acceptance than have the others. The first of these stories, although it lacks great significance, shows with what seriousness Voltaire's detractors would make themselves ridiculous while attempting to cast disparagement upon his name. The incident, reported by Ruffhead in his *Life of Pope*, was first printed in 1769.

" Mr. Pope told one of his most intimate friends that the poet Voltaire had got some recommendation to him when he came to England, and that the first time he saw him was at Twickenham, where he kept him to dinner. Mrs. Pope, an excellent woman, was then alive, and observing that this stranger, who appeared to be entirely emaciated, had no stomach, she expressed her concern for his want of appetite, on which Voltaire gave her so indelicate and brutal an account of the occasion of his disorder, contracted in Italy, that the poor lady was obliged immediately to rise from the table. When Mr. Pope related that, his friend asked him how he could forbear ordering his servant John to thrust Voltaire head and shoulders out of his house? He replied that there was more ignorance in his conduct than a purposed affront; that Voltaire came into England, as other foreigners do, on a prepossession that not only all religion, but all common decency of morals, was lost among us." [1]

Dr. Johnson's version of the story, undoubtedly taken from Ruffhead, has improved with age:

" In the year 1726, Voltaire, having visited England, was introduced to Mr. Pope. Being invited to dine with him, he talked at the table with such combined indecency and blasphemy, as compelled Mr. Pope's mother, with disgust and horror, to leave the company. Pope disrelished Voltaire from that time; and soon found that the blasphemer of his Creator was equally deficient in honour and integrity as in piety." [2]

That Voltaire, fresh from the most exclusive society in France and accustomed to daily intercourse with the elegant and polite Parisian world, should be guilty of such conduct is sufficiently unaccountable. Yet that he should behave in such a manner upon his introduction to the great English poet whom he already admired and whose company he eagerly sought, is beyond belief. Voltaire, of all people, had the polite ability to ingratiate himself to those whom he admired; never could he have been guilty of such coarse clumsiness. One need not point out that it would have been impossible for him to have brought back from Italy any physical disorder, as he had never been in that country; or to show that at this time his fluency in English was not great enough to allow him to commit such a blunder. The entire incident is ridiculous and impossible.

Another story of Voltaire's relations with Pope is more

[1] Ruffhead, *Life of Pope*, 213, n. [2] *Addisoniana*, Vol. II, p. 34.

serious in its implication, and, at first glance, seems well supported by circumstantial evidence. It accuses Voltaire of the vilest sort of duplicity and, if proved, would establish him as a petty parasite and traitor. In December, 1726, Bolingbroke and Pulteny founded the *Craftsman*, which soon became famous for the vigor of its opposition to Walpole's policies. Within two months they had launched a new attack in the form of a pamphlet entitled, *The Occasional Writer*. Written with piercing irony and perfection of style, this attack upon Walpole made a great stir in London. Voltaire's supposed connection with it forms our second story. This anecdote, too, is first told by Ruffhead, who got it from Warburton.

"Mr. Pope said . . . that Voltaire was a spy for the court while he stayed in England; of which he gave his friend the following instance: When the first *Occasional Letter* to Sir Robert Walpole came out . . . he [Voltaire] made Mr. Pope a visit at Twickenham; and walking with him in his garden he said: Pope, this *Occasional Letter* alarms the Court extremely. It is finely written. As you converse much with the best pens conversant in public business, you must know the author. You may safely tell this secret to a stranger, who has no concern with your national quarrels. Mr. Pope said, he perfectly understood him as he knew his character; and, to make trial, which hardly needed any, he replied: Mr. Voltaire, you are a man of honour; I may safely, I know, trust an important secret to your breast. I myself wrote it. Voltaire, after launching out into high encomiums on the performance, was, he perceived, impatient to get away; and the next day he [Pope] heard that all the court reported that he was the author. This infamy of the man gave Mr. Pope and his friends much occasion of mirth, and much light in the manner how he ought to be treated." [3]

This malignant gossip, coming, as did the other story about Voltaire's connection with Pope, from Warburton through Ruffhead's *Life of Pope*, might easily be discounted on the ground of the enmity of its originator and the fact that it did not appear until more than forty years after the event was supposed to have taken place. Warburton is known to have had a quarrel with the author of the *Henriade* which left him bitter against Voltaire.[4] His animosity is shown in a letter in which he refers to Voltaire as a scoundrel.[5] Two points, however, have served to strengthen Warburton's report. In the first place it is an undoubted fact that Voltaire was on terms of intimacy both with members of Walpole's party and with Bolingbroke and other members of the opposition. Secondly, many people are ready to believe such behavior strictly in keeping with his character. So generally is such an estimate of Voltaire accepted outside of France that a critic of the caliber of Churton Collins, in summing up this Voltaire-Pope episode, gives way to an outburst like the following:

" Throughout his aims were purely selfish, and to obtain his ends he resorted to means which no man of an honest and independent spirit would have stooped to use. It would perhaps be unduly harsh to describe him as a parasite and a sycophant; but it is nevertheless true that he too often figures in a character bordering on both. His

---

[3] Ruffhead, *op. cit.*, p. 214, n.
[4] Foulet, *op. cit.*, p. 259.
[5] Warburton, *Letters*, p. 466.

correspondence — and his conversation no doubt resembled his correspondence — is almost sickening. His compliments are so fulsome, his flattery so exaggerated, that they might excusably be taken for elaborate irony. He seems to be always on his knees. There was scarcely a distinguished man then living in England who had not been the object of this nauseous homage. He pours it indiscriminately on Pope, Swift, Gay, Clarke, on half the Cabinet and on half the peerage. In a man of this character, falsehood and hypocrisy are of the very essence of his composition. There is nothing, however base, to which he will not stoop; there is no law in the code of social honour which he is not capable of violating. . . . Another disagreeable trait in Voltaire's social character was the gross impropriety of his conversation, even in the presence of those whose age and sex should have been sufficient protection from such annoyance." [6] When, in a book of serious criticism, purporting to be impartial and sympathetic, one encounters a passage like this, the danger of permitting to go unchallenged such attacks upon Voltaire is apparent. It is largely upon stories of this kind that such attacks can be based. Let us, then, examine Warburton's anecdote in detail.

As its very essence, this story presupposes that the author of the *Occasional Writer* was unknown to Walpole, and that he was forced to resort to a spy in his attempt to find out who wrote it. An examination of the facts will easily disprove this. Although the pamphlet was printed anonymously, public opinion had at once named its author, and named him correctly. No one but Bolingbroke could

[6] Churton Collins, *op. cit.*, p. 44.

have composed such a masterpiece, and letters and pamphlets of the time universally attribute it to him. To suppose that the Prime Minister was ignorant of a fact that was the gossip of all London is absurd. Besides, we have concrete evidence that Walpole knew the author of this attack upon him. Ten days after the appearance of the *Occasional Writer* there was printed an answer to it entitled, *A Letter to the Occasional Writer,* which was undoubtedly written either by Walpole himself or by someone under his direction. No name was mentioned in this reply, but there could not be the slightest doubt as to who was addressed. A sentence like the following one could apply only to Bolingbroke: " I know that you love the Emperor because he reasembles you in his ingratitude, and you detest the French merely because they received you so well." [7] Except for Warburton's story there is no evidence that Pope was ever suspected of having written this pamphlet, and, indeed, it is hard to believe that Pope, abandoning his couplets, would produce prose in the style of this article. Thus it is apparent that, as Walpole knew from the first that Bolingbroke was the author of the attack, he would not have employed Voltaire to secure this information for him, and Warburton's accusation fails before it has started.

Although Warburton's accusation is so easily discredited, there still lingers by inference a suspicion of double dealing and treachery on the part of Voltaire. An attempt to find the basic reason for such a charge, throws some light upon the nature of Voltaire's position in England.

---

[7] Foulet, *op. cit.,* p. 260 (this has been re-translated from the French).

One has but to read the polemics of the period to sense the bitterness of political strife in England. Because of Walpole's overwhelming and obedient majority in Parliament, this struggle was temporarily bereft of practical significance, but the traditional antagonism continued unchecked. Whig continued to hate Tory with that blind and bigoted tenacity, handed down from one generation to the next, which has characterized the history of the party system in Anglo-Saxon countries. It was detestable to Voltaire to see such bigotry in an otherwise tolerant land. The senseless antagonism between Whigs and Tories distressed him. He steadfastly refused to be a party to it, and did his best to ignore its existence. Speaking of the violence of English party spirit, he says in the *Lettres Philosophiques*, "One half of the nation is always the enemy of the other half. I found people who assured me that Lord Marlborough was a poltroon and that Mr. Pope was a fool, just as in France some of the Jesuits think Pascal a nitwit, and some of the Jansenists say that Father Bourdaloue was nothing but a babbler. To the Jacobites Mary Stuart is a saint and a heroine; to the rest of the people she is a debauché, an adulteress, an homicide." [8]

For Voltaire the arbitrary barriers of party did not exist. He was making an exhaustive study of England and of the English people, not of Whigs or Tories. Voltaire was interested in these divisions as they afforded him an opportunity to learn the characteristics of the English people, but he realized that he could not get an accurate and impartial idea of the English if he saw only members of one party. As he pointed out in the *Lettres Philosophiques*,

[8] Voltaire, *Lettres Philosophiques*, Letter XXII, translated.

in England there were always partisan statements on any given political question; never was there impartial display and discussion of the facts. Consequently, from the first Voltaire had been careful to make friends with distinguished men in both parties. He saw no reason why he should not be on equally good terms with Bolingbroke and Pope, and with Walpole and Dodington. In his social intercourse he attempted to ignore their political enmity.

At a time when political antagonism was so strong, it seems inevitable that both parties should want this distinguished foreigner to side with them. Some went farther than to lament the fact that their party did not have Voltaire's unqualified support: They felt that anyone who was not whole-heartedly on their side must be against them, and as a result members of each party suspected that Voltaire was secretly in league with their enemies. They could not realize that there were those to whom this partisan strife was ridiculous and the predominance of one party a matter of slight importance. With some such preconceived opinion, it was a simple matter for Warburton to fabricate a concrete example of Voltaire's treachery, sure in his heart that his conclusions were correct, even if his facts were not.

It is possible that Warburton's two stories about Voltaire were not intentional attempts to slander the Frenchman. The stories appeared at a time when Voltaire's very name was detested, and Warburton's personal dislike for Voltaire may have convinced him that his anecdotes gave a true impression of Voltaire's character.

The grave danger of such a practice as this is shown

by two stories that appeared thirty years after Warburton's, apparently based upon these same premises. An anonymous correspondent of *The Gentleman's Magazine* wrote the following story to that paper. Prefacing his remarks with the assurance that he has the information, " on very good authority," he says:

" Voltaire, when in London, was very intimate with Pope; he was familiar at his table, and introduced to the circle of his acquaintance. But Gratitude, and a respect for the laws of Hospitality, make no part of the morality of Infidels. What did this mean poltroon do, but one day, when he knew the Poet was from home, he called on his ancient mother, who lived with him, and told her that he should be very sorry to do anything to displease her, but really it was so hard living in London, that he had a poem, a severe lampoon upon her, which he was going to publish, but would recommend it to her to give him a sum of money to suppress it. The fear of the poor old woman at length prevailed over her indignation, and she bribed him not to publish; which he agreed to do on one condition, that she should never mention the subject. She promised, and she kept her word. Having succeeded so well once he made a second attempt on such an easy prey. Whether he applied again too soon, or her indignation was not subsided, but Pope came in at that moment. His mother was in a violent and uncommon passion; and he insisted to know the cause. She informed him, as well as she could for rage and indignation. Voltaire had neither time to make off, nor to frame some lie for his excuse; when the little man, who was never wanting in filial respect, flew with violence on the long, lank Frenchman, striking him with all the rage that honest indignation could supply him with. Voltaire, in attempting to make a precipitate retreat, fell over a chair. It is needless to observe that there ceased his connection with our poet." [9]

Is it too much to suspect that this minutely descriptive story is merely an artistic variant of Ruffhead's original anecdote about Voltaire and Mrs. Pope? Surely it is more to the point to accuse Voltaire of blackmailing a helpless widow, than merely of forcing her out of the room by his vile language. And how much more dramatic it is for the weak and crippled Pope to drive Voltaire stumbling from the house, instead of calmly listening to his profanity! One must admit that the original form of the story is much less effective than the last.

Conclusive proof that there were not unpleasant relations between Pope and Voltaire is the fact that they always remained good friends, and continued to admire each other. If incidents such as these had actually occurred, who can imagine the ironic and over-sensitive author of the *Dunciad* failing to take revenge in a fiery couplet? And would Voltaire, who could not resist attacking with all his virulence any petty scribbler who happened to take him to task, fail to send home a stinging sarcasm to Pope? Neither of these writers would have had the restraint to conceal his enmity, if there had been any. Happily there is no evidence that the relations between them were anything but cordial. In the solitude of their retreat at Cirey, Voltaire often spoke in praise of Pope to the Marquise du Châtelet. The divine Emile corresponded regularly with Twickenham, and upon one occasion she wrote to Pope

[9] *The Gentleman's Magazine*, 1797, Vol. LXVII, Part II, p. 1009.

that Voltaire " has always spoken to me about you with infinite esteem."

We can now turn to the last story. An anonymous corre- spondent of *The Gentleman's Magazine,* writing seventy years after Voltaire's departure from England, depicts with the greatest detail Voltaire's precipitate flight from England at the point of Lord Peterborough's sword. " He *very* narrowly," says this amusing author, " escaped being suddenly dismissed from ENGLAND TO HELL." The story is as follows: Lord Peterborough had employed Voltaire to write and publish a certain book for him, and had con- stantly supplied him with money for this purpose. This money Voltaire kept for himself, refusing to advance more than ten pounds to the printer, who was finally forced to stop work from lack of funds. To Peter- borough's inquiries about the book Voltaire replied that English printers were very dilatory, and to the printer he said that his lordship would advance no more money until the completion of the book. Finally, suspecting Voltaire of duplicity, the printer went directly to Peterborough, and finding him walking in his garden at Parson's Green, he informed him of Voltaire's actions.

" Any attempt to describe Lord P.'s indignation exceeds *mortal* powers; he did, however, at length utter, THE VILLAIN! At that instant Voltaire appeared at the end of a very long gravel-walk. Lord P. exclaimed: " Here he comes, and I will *kill* him *instantly.*" So saying, he drew his sword and ran like lightning. Happily, or perhaps un- happily, for the wretch Voltaire, Mr. St. André, then present, caught Lord P. in his arms, exclaiming: ' Good God! my lord, if you murder him, you will be hanged.'

'*I care not for that*; I WILL KILL THE VILLAIN!' The walk being one of the old-fashioned King William garden-walks, very long, Voltaire proceeded some way before he descried the London bookseller. At the moment Mr. St. André screamed out: 'Fly for your life, for I cannot hold my Lord many moments longer.' And he declared to my friend that, young and strong, the hero neither [*sic*], yet invigorated by his extreme indignation, it was with his utmost exertions that he confined him, his sword drawn in one hand, which he would not drop, hoping to escape, and, as he said, plunge it into his vile heart. He broke loose; but love of life had given wings to the worse than fiend — he fled, concealed himself that night in a village, went the next day to London, and proceeded immediately to the Continent, leaving his portmanteau, papers, etc., at Lord Peterborough's. He went without a hat — whether he strolled into the garden without it, or that it fell in his flight, I do not recollect." [10]

The exact detail of this description seems to make its accuracy unquestionable. Certainly if this eye witness is sure enough of his facts to be able to state definitely that Voltaire left Peterborough's garden without a hat, he cannot be mistaken as to the major points of his story! Unfortunately for this anonymous artist's desire to defame Voltaire, Lord Peterborough himself contradicts him. We have a letter from Peterborough written a month after Voltaire's departure from England, in which he refers to that event. " It is as hard," he says, " to account for our politics as for Mr. Voltaire's resolutions and conduct; the country and the people of England are

[10] *The Gentleman's Magazine*, October, 1797, Vol. LXVII, Part II.

in disgrace at present, and [he] has taken his leave of us, as a foolish people who believe in God and trust in ministers; and he is gone to Constantinople in order to believe in the Gospels, which he says it is impossible to do living among the teachers of Christianity." [11] This, certainly, is not the tone of a man whose one desire a month before was to run his sword through Voltaire. There is not the slightest touch of personal resentment in this letter. We must, I fear, judge that the correspondent of *The Gentleman's Magazine* has ascribed to Lord Peterborough sentiments that he himself felt.

It is unfortunate that of the few anecdotes which we possess concerning Voltaire's stay in England, so many should have been devoted to malicious attempts at slander. This is doubly to be regretted because, not only do these attacks give an erroneous idea of the nature of Voltaire's relations with Englishmen, but there are so few concrete facts with which to counterbalance the fallacious impression thus conveyed. Our knowledge of Voltaire's intercourse with the English is dependent upon a circuitous analysis of the character and reactions of Voltaire and of his English friends, and the piecing together of fragmentary facts and anecdotes. Perhaps we should consider ourselves fortunate that there is material enough available to enable us to refute envious attacks upon him. The loss of Voltaire's personal diaries and note-books, the destruction of his voluminous correspondence with Bolingbroke, and the loss of so many of his letters to other Englishmen, combined with the fact that there is so little reference to him by contemporary English writers, make

[11] Foulet, *op. cit.*, p. 178.

practically impossible an accurate and detailed biography of this portion of his life.

How fortunate we should be had a Boswell accompanied Voltaire to England! It is tantalizing to imagine the wealth of anecdote, of sparkling wit, of incisive criticism and discussion that might have been recorded had such a person been present at Voltaire's meetings with distinguished Englishmen. From parenthetical sentences here and there we find that he spent three months with Lord Peterborough at his country place, where Swift was among the members of the distinguished party; when he visited Dodington he met Young, Thomson, and other celebrated Whigs; at another party at the Earl of Temple's country seat Pope was among the guests. While he was making his début in London society in 1726, Voltaire had an opportunity to meet and converse with most of the prominent Englishmen of the time; but it was at these protracted house parties with Peterborough, Dodington, and others, that he became intimately acquainted with them, and that he acquired his great knowledge and understanding of English character and culture. M. Lanson, in his exhaustive and scholarly edition of Voltaire's *Lettres Philosophiques,* has put on record books from which Voltaire might have obtained the material for almost every sentence in that epoch-making book. One feels sure, however, that if there existed stenographic reports of Voltaire's conversations at these various house-parties, the sources, not only of the *Lettres Philosophiques,* but of Voltaire's entire knowledge of English would be apparent.

Amid the splendor of Bolingbroke's London house,

over the velvet expanse of Peterborough's famous lawns, in the grandeur of Dodington's estate at Eastbury, Voltaire, surrounded by brilliant wits and thinkers, first became imbued with the cosmopolitan ideal. He was equipped with a perfect understanding of the spirit that had placed France in her preëminent position in the literary world, yet his breadth of sympathy made him the first of his nation really to appreciate the English genius, so vastly different from the French in its aims and methods. What would one not give to have a complete report of the discussions and comparisons of France and England from the mouths of Voltaire and his English friends! What masterpieces of wit and penetration have been lost through the failure to record the discussions of those master satirists, Swift, Voltaire, Pope, and Bolingbroke! What a wealth of material for a study of the growth of Voltaire's ideas lies wasted in the buried memory of those immortal Englishmen! One can picture the lank, emaciated Frenchman, his eyes burning with startling intensity, surrounded by a circle of distinguished Englishmen, here making an ironic thrust, there parrying with a sudden twist a menacing attack, his keen mind playing intensely, yet wittily, over the whole range of human thought, and, as the discussion warms, there appears on his face that sardonic smile which is as much a part of him as his sensitiveness or his wit. Lightly he skims the surface of poetry from Homer to Milton. With deft thrusts he exposes the salient points of Corneille and of Shakespeare, making them both ridiculous, then with a quick thrust bringing out their different geniuses. Drawing out the convictions of his companions, he turns the conversation to religion and to philosophy,

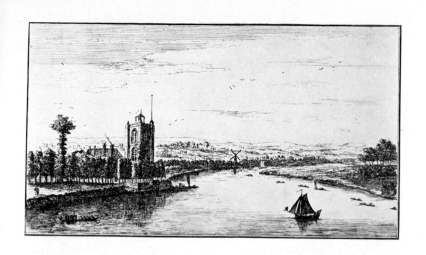

A View of the Celebrated Mr. Pope's House at Twickenham

ENGLISH COUNTRY SCENES: WANDSWORTH REACH AND POPE'S HOUSE
AT TWICKENHAM

and the strength and weakness of all systems are laid bare. And through the varied rhythm of their witty discourses runs as a directing power Voltaire's insatiable curiosity, his unending search for truth by means of an examination of human experience.

A few scattered anecdotes which have been handed down allow momentary glimpses behind the closed curtain of Voltaire's life in England. Croft, in his *Life of Young*, gives the following incident about Voltaire's life at Eastbury. Dodington's guests were indulging in a discussion of Milton's *Paradise Lost*, Young praising the poem, while Voltaire pointed out its weaknesses. " Voltaire, who had as little sympathy with Milton as he had with Aeschylus and Dante, objected to the episode of Sin and Death, contending that as they were abstractions it was absurd to assign them offices proper only to concrete beings. These objections he enforced with his usual eloquence and sarcastic wit. The parallel between the hungry monster of Milton, ' grinning horrible ' its ' ghastly smile,' and the meagre form of the speaker — his thin face lighted up, as it always was in conversation, with that peculiar sardonic smile familiar to us from his portraits — was irresistible. And Young closed the argument with an epigram:

> ' *You are so witty, profligate, and thin,*
> *At once we think thee Milton, Death, and Sin.*' " [12]

Years later in his poem entitled *Sea Piece*, which he dedicated to Voltaire, Young evidently refers to this discussion, in which he flatters himself that he convinced the Frenchman of Milton's genius:

[12] Collins, *op. cit.*, p. 31.

[161]

" Tell me," say'st thou, " who courts my smile?
What stranger strayed from yonder isle? "
No stranger, sir! tho' born in foreign climes;
On Dorset downs, when Milton's page,
With Sin *and* Death, *provok'd thy rage,*
Thy rage provok'd who sooth'd with gentle rhyme?

Who kindly couch'd thy censure's eye,
And gave thee clearly to descrie
Sound judgment giving laws to fancy strong?
Who half inclin'd thee to confess,
Nor could thy modesty do less.
That Milton's blindness lay not in his song?

The well-known incident of his meeting with Congreve
cannot be omitted from an account of Voltaire's visit to
England. Voltaire thought highly of Congreve's plays.
" He has written but few plays," says Voltaire in the
Lettres Philosophiques, " but they are all excellent of
their kind. They, rigorously observe the rules of the
theatre. They are full of characters shaded off with extreme delicacy. They contain no false wit; the language
everywhere is that of honorable people though the actions
are those of knaves: and this proves that Congreve knew
well the people he had to deal with, and that he lived in
what is called good society." Having such an opinion of
his plays, Voltaire was prepared to be delighted with Congreve's personality. But Congreve, gouty, blind, on the
verge of death, was unbearably affected. He pretended
that his renown was due to his character as a gentleman,
and that his plays were unimportant bagatelles, thrown off

in caprice. " He was," says Voltaire, "infirm and nearly dying when I knew him. He had one defect: he did not sufficiently esteem his profession of authorship, which had made his reputation and his fortune. He spoke to me of his works as trifles which were beneath his notice, and in our first conversation he told me to look upon him merely as a gentleman who lived a very simple life. I replied that if he had had the misfortune of being only a gentleman like any other, I would never have come to see him. I was shocked at vanity so out of place." [13]

To Congreve he may have owed his introduction to the Dowager Duchess of Marlborough, whom he visited at Blenheim. Two stories, told, it is true, on no very satisfactory authority, but so probable in character that one is inclined to accept them, connect Voltaire with the Duchess of Marlborough's *Memoires*, which was being written at this time. Duvernet, Voltaire's first biographer, relates that when Voltaire asked permission to see part of the manuscript of the *Memoires*, the Duchess said to him, " Wait a little, I am at present altering my account of Queen Anne's character; I have begun to love her again since the present lot have become our governors." The other story, told by Goldsmith in his *Life of Voltaire*, shows us that Voltaire's surprises, as he discovered the character of the English, were not all pleasant.

" Among . . . those who either patronized him [Voltaire], or enrolled themselves in the list of his friends, was the Duchess of Marlborough. She found infinite pleasure in the agreeable vivacity of his conversation; but mistook his levity for want of principle. Such a man

[13] Voltaire, *Lettres Philosophiques*, Letter XIX, translated.

seemed to her the properest person to digest the *Memoires* of her life; which, even so early as this, she had an inclination of publishing. She proposed the task accordingly to him, and he readily undertook to oblige her. But when she showed him her materials, and began to dictate the use she would have them turned to, Voltaire appeared no longer the good-natured, complying creature which she took him for. He found some characters were to be blackened without just ground, some of her actions to be vindicated that deserved censure, and a mistress to be exposed to whom she owed infinite obligations. Our poet accordingly remonstrated with her Grace, and seemed to intimate the inconsistency of such conduct with gratitude and justice. He gravely assured her that the publication of secrets which were communicated to her under the seal of friendship would give the world no high opinion of her morals. He was thus continuing his discourse, when the Duchess, quite in a passion, snatched the papers out of his hands. I thought, she said, the man had sense; but I find him at bottom either a fool or a philosopher." [14]

If the authenticity of this incident could be definitely established, it would go far toward destroying the unfortunate legend of Voltaire's knavery and willingness to stoop to the most disreputable means of gaining money and prestige. Unhappily Goldsmith mentions no authority for the story, and no one else has repeated it.

Little is known of Voltaire's relations with English ladies, although his reference to the tendency of Frenchmen to be repulsed by " the coldness, and the icy and disdainful airs with which English ladies begin every ac-

[14] Goldsmith, *Works*, IV, 24.

quaintance, and from which some of them never free themselves," leads one to suspect that in English ladies Voltaire missed the warmth and the spontaneity which characterized their French sisters. Besides his enlightening experience with the Duchess of Marlborough, we have definite information about his connection with only two other English ladies. That he was one of the thousand admirers of the most popular woman of that age — Molly Lepel — is attested by the fact that his only poem in English now in existence is addressed to her. If the mediocrity of his verses measures the extent of his passion, one might well believe that Voltaire's professed love for Lord Hervey's wife was merely another attempt on his part to be fashionable.

" *Hervey, would you know the passion*
 You have kindl'd in my breast?
Trifling is the inclination
 That by words can be express'd.

In my silence see the lover —
 True love is best by silence known;
In my eyes you'll best discover
 All the power of your own."

A letter written by Voltaire to Mrs. Clayton — the influential Lady Sundon of George II's court — gives us a glimpse of Voltaire's usual attitude toward English ladies. " Tho' I am out of London,' writes Voltaire, " the favours your ladyship has honoured me with, are not, nor will ever be out of my memory. I'll remember as long as I live, that the most respectable lady who waits, and is a friend, of the most truly great queen in the world, has vouchsafed, to protect me and receive me with kindness while I was at London. I am just now arrived at Paris, and I pay my respects to your court, before I see our own. I wish for the honour of Versailles, and for the improvement of virtue and letters we could have here some ladyes like you. You see my wishes are unbounded." Although Voltaire probably found English ladies personally somewhat unattractive, he was politely attentive to those whose influence might be useful to him. His graceful French flattery, contrasting so strikingly with the brusque indifference of the English court, was undoubtedly most pleasing to those who were so favored.

CHAPTER TEN
THE SHAKESPEARE PARADOX

CHAPTER TEN

THE SHAKESPEARE PARADOX

OFTEN it is in history that we seek relief from the complexity of life. If we cannot comprehend the subtle and contradictory qualities of our neighbors, or even of ourselves, at least in history we shall find direct and simplified issues. That we may do so, life has to be simplified out of all relation to reality, but that is a minor consideration as long as we are reassured that living is not such a difficult matter after all. The historian who cannot take his place definitely on one side of a question or on another is unsatisfactory. Somehow, we feel, he cannot be very capable.

Voltaire's reputation has suffered from this popular desire for condensing. It is undeniable that he attacked the Catholic Church; some of his diatribes may be equally applied to all Christian sects. Therefore he is a blasphemous atheist and an adherent of immorality. The classification is easy to remember; we may proceed to the next one. The facility with which such labels may be applied makes it difficult to tear them off, unless one can discover a label equally simple — and, often, equally fallacious.

The facts of the case are plain. Voltaire was rash enough to attack Shakespeare; some of his comments on the English dramatist are ridiculous and absurd. The answer, therefore, is easy: Voltaire had not the slightest

appreciation of Shakespeare's genius; his critical astute-
ness has been over-rated. There is just one inconvenient
obstacle in the way of the application of this formula. It
happens that Voltaire was the first person to call the attention of Europe to Shakespeare's genius. Before the
publication of the *Lettres Philosophiques*, Shakespeare's
very name was unknown outside of England; after 1733
no cultivated European could afford to be without an
opinion about him. And so the task of simplification begins
once again. The conclusion remains unchanged; it is
merely necessary to rearrange the premises. It is assumed
that Voltaire changed his mind. When he wrote the letter
on Shakespeare in the *Lettres Philosophiques*, either out
of a desire to please the English, or to shock the French,
or merely to be sensational (the "why" is not really
important), he praised the English dramatist. Later, when
free from English influence, his true character showed
itself and he began his monstrous attacks. The formula
remains unchanged.

It is worth the effort of attempting to get an accurate
estimate of Voltaire's reactions to Shakespeare, if for no
other reason, merely because of the light that is thrown
upon Voltaire's character and upon the limits of his genius.
To do this it is first necessary to know the conditions under
which he became acquainted with Shakespeare.

The history of Shakespeare's influence upon the Continent is more than the satisfaction of idle curiosity as to
the reception given a great genius by various peoples; it is
more than a record of appreciation or of disapproval. It is
intimately connected with the record of active literary
development in Europe for more than two centuries. It is

a key to innate racial differences. It is a standard for the comparison of the native genius of various countries. In Germany the influence of Shakespeare fell upon fertile ground, in France upon barren rock; but the story of the frustrated efforts of the Shakespearian seed as it attempted to send its roots into the meagre soil of classical France is as interesting and as instructive as the history of the luxuriant plant in Germany, with its roots firmly implanted in the most fertile soil of German literature.

In France, from the first Shakespeare had to contend with a people who were loth to acknowledge foreign excellence of any kind unlike their own, and with a society whose mental habits, firm and imperious, made it almost impossible for it to be sympathetic to his genius. The French demanded logic, conciseness, simplicity. They were moved by the subtle analysis of a Racine, progressing from point to point with the inevitableness of a syllogism. They were charmed by clarity and order; the very atmosphere of decorum and restraint of the classical tragedy moved them. But they were soon bored by the vivid, colorful contrasts of English poetic language; their feeling for restraint was as easily offended by flights of fancy as by brutal realism. Instead of classic "types," Shakespeare created individuals, complex, subtle, impulsive, and ever changing. His characters seemed vague and indeterminate to the French. In discussing Voltaire's reactions to Shakespeare, we must constantly keep in sight this difference between the literary tastes of the two peoples.

When Voltaire went to England neither he nor any other Frenchman had more than the vaguest knowledge of Shakespeare.[1] It never occurred to Frenchmen that there could exist a method of writing tragedy even remotely comparable to that of the French classical tradition. Feeling as they did that the doctrine of the unities was the great discovery in dramatic art whereby a playwright was guided in the most effective presentation of his material, the French considered an author writing without the advantages of this system to be hopelessly handicapped.[2] Voltaire's apprenticeship as a playwright was spent in the mastery of the classical rules. Never had he complained of their restrictions; he had been thankful for their guidance. The unexampled success of his play, *Oedipe*, was largely due to the aid of these rules. Not only was Voltaire's whole background inseparably connected with the classical tradition, but his success as a dramatist placed upon him a personal responsibility for the great French tradition. If any movement against it were to appear Voltaire would be looked upon as its outstanding defender.

When Voltaire reached England he discovered that most of the distinguished English critics belittled their great dramatist. They felt that, had Shakespeare enjoyed the aid of the rules of the French classical tradition, he would have ranked among the world's great dramatists. As it was, they could only admire those particular passages

[1] M. Baldensperger's discovery that the quarto editions of Shakespeare's plays which found their way to Paris were valued at one sou each tells us more about Shakespeare's reputation before Voltaire than the erudite discussions as to what Frenchman was the first to mention the English dramatist's name, Baldensperger, *Études d'Histoire Littéraire*, 2ᵉ série, p. 156, *Esquisse d'une Histoire de Shakespeare en France.*

[2] Although Voltaire defended the classical tradition with the greatest vehemence throughout his life, he thought the doctrine of the unities to be the essential point in that system, and he was willing that the other rules should be relaxed.

in his plays in which he did not offend their sense of the appropriate. Shaftesbury liked Shakespeare in spite of " his natural rudeness, his unpolished style, his antiquated phrase and wit, his want of method and coherence, his deficiency in almost all the graces and ornaments of this kind of writing." [3] Pope, one of Shakespeare's most enthusiastic supporters, remarked: " It must be owned that with all these great excellencies he had almost as great defects; and that as he has certainly written better, so he has perhaps written worse, than any other." [4] John Dennis, a prominent critic, said of Shakespeare, " If he had had the advantage of Art and Learning, he would have surpassed the very best and strongest of the Ancients." [5] Bolingbroke believed that the English did not possess a single good tragedy, and Chesterfield ridiculed Shakespeare. Thus, Voltaire could have ignored Shakespeare's claim to greatness with the backing of the most important section of English critical opinion. It would not have been unexpected had Voltaire never given him more than a moment's notice.

Surprisingly, Shakespeare swept Voltaire off his feet. Although Voltaire never thought of quitting the firm foundation of the French classical tradition, he suddenly saw, as he thought, a great opportunity to improve it. Just as the contrast of English political institutions to those of France had clarified his thoughts on government, so the contrast of Shakespeare to the French dramatists gave him a new basis for criticizing French tragedy. The comparison left him with a clear realization of shortcomings in the

[3] Shaftesbury, *Advice to an Author*, Part II, sec. 3.
[4] Pope, *Preface to an Edition of Shakespeare*, London, 1725.
[5] Dennis, *On the Genius and Writings of Shakespeare*, London, 1711.

French dramatic tradition. He soon felt the lack of action, the absence of dramatic stimulus in contemporary French plays. The monotonous regularity of the verses; the conventionalized, almost symbolic, expression of passion, the excessive use of the love motif; the substitution of long, dull monologues for conversation and action; the relegation of the most striking scenes to the *coulisses;* the unwavering respect for the fastidious "rules of decency"; the lack of movement and color; the use of indirect description in the place of direct portrayal; and the general preoccupation of French dramatists with the avoidance of "irregularities" instead of the securing of dramatic effects, were apparent to Voltaire.

The qualities in Shakespeare's plays that attracted Voltaire were their immense vitality and vividness, their continual action, their fire, their color. The manner in which Shakespeare swept his characters so irresistibly through their emotional crises forced Voltaire to forget for the moment the unorthodox manner in which these effects were secured. When Voltaire saw Shakespeare's plays presented, he was brought face to face with the fact that here, without the supposedly essential aid of the classical rules, were living characters carried intensely through a play by the power of convincing dramatic action. He had always supposed that a play which disregarded the rules would have its dramatic interest so widely disseminated that there could remain no absorbing plot. Yet in Shakespeare's plays he found dramatic interest which was distinctly superior to that in most French tragedies. The realization was disconcerting, yet, with that honesty which always kept him from attempting to avoid a fact, Voltaire tried to reconcile his knowledge of the dramatic power of Shakespeare with his unshaken belief in the essential soundness of the unities.

It was here that Voltaire betrayed his lack of critical insight. He was moved by Shakespeare's plays, yet when he measured them by the rules of the dramatic tradition to which he was accustomed, they appeared to be worthless. In consequence he disregarded them as plays. He decided that this ignorant writer, this charlatan Shakespeare, had somehow stumbled upon a series of successful dramatic tricks. He attempted to discover these " tricks " in hopes that he could include them within the arbitrary boundaries of his dramatic convention. He was seeking in purely incidental matters the cause of Shakespeare's greatness as a dramatist.

As a result, when Voltaire introduced Shakespeare into France he had no interest in communicating to the French the fact that they, had ignored a great lyric poet; he himself scarcely recognized this side of Shakespeare's genius. He was introducing not a man, not a poet, but an influence. It is essential to remember this if we desire to understand Voltaire's attitude toward Shakespeare. He did not seek to enjoy Shakespeare, but to make use of him, to add the discoveries of this powerful, but ignorant and untrained genius, to the rich store of the French tradition.

In the *Discours sur la tragédie*, which was published as a preface to *Brutus*, Voltaire first brought his new discovery to the attention of the French. As if to emphasize the English influence which was being introduced, the essay is in the form of an epistle to Lord Bolingbroke in which Voltaire compares the French and the English dra-

matic conventions. In the first part of the essay Voltaire
admits that on his return to France he was alarmed at the
severity of French poetic laws and especially at the absolute slavery of the French to rhyme. " I missed," he tells
Bolingbroke, " that happy lack of restriction which allows
you to write tragedy in unrhymed verse; to lengthen and,
especially, to shorten almost any word; to run a verse
over from one line to another; and, when necessity demands it, to create new words which when they are
sonorous, intelligent and necessary, are adopted into the
language. 'A poet,' I said, 'is a free man who forces
language to be slave to his genius. A Frenchman is a slave
to rhyme, sometimes obliged to write four verses to express a thought which an Englishman could give in a
single line. The Englishman says what he wants to, the
Frenchman only what he is able to; the one runs in a
vast race-course, the other walks in fetters on a narrow
and slippery road!'"

Here, one feels, Voltaire is on the verge of revolting
against the too restrictive rules of French dramatic composition. But immediately his tone changes. He feels that
he has gone far enough in his criticism of the French
dramatic convention, so he gives several reasons for the
restrictions placed upon French dramatists. He argues that
the French language is such that in it one cannot tell the
difference between prose and poetry except for rhyme.
And in closing his half-hearted defense of the narrow
French tradition, he claims that the great writers have so
accustomed French audiences to the harmony of rhymed
verse that they will bear no other form. " Whoever would
free himself," says Voltaire, " from a burden which the

great Corneille bore would be thought of, and rightly so, not as a bold genius, opening a new path for us, but as a weakling, unable to continue in the path trod by the ancients. . . . We do not allow the slightest license; we demand of an author that he shall ever be bound by all these chains, yet that he shall always have the appearance of being free. We recognize as poets only those who fulfill all these conditions."

This form of exposition was a favorite one with Voltaire. He would first present striking arguments against the institution which he was attacking. Later, to safeguard himself from attack, he would repeat in an unconvincing way the arguments which were likely to be brought to the defense of the object of his attack. In this way he preserved a semblance of impartiality at the same time that he disarmed his opponents.

Thus Voltaire gave the impression of closing the door leading to more liberal verse form in French dramatic writing. His tentative opening of that door had given French writers a momentary glimpse into a new environment and had fixed its existence in their minds.

Having disposed of this problem, he prepared to face another question brought up by the contrast of English and French tragedy. " Being unable, my lord," says Voltaire, " to venture unrhymed verse on the French stage, much as one might do in Italy or in England, I wished at least to bring to our theatre certain of the beauties which yours possesses. It is true, I admit, that there are many faults in the English theatre. But in recompense, in those monstrous plays of yours there are admirable scenes. Up to the present time almost all of the tragic authors in your country have lacked the purity, the order, the decorous plot and style, the elegance, and all of those other fine points in dramatic art which have established the preëminent reputation of the French theatre since the great Corneille. But the most irregular of your plays possess one great merit, that of action.

"In France we have well-thought-of plays which are rather conversations than the portrayal of an actual event. . . . Our excessive delicacy forces us sometimes to put in the form of narrative things which we would prefer to expose before the eyes of the audience. We are afraid to put on the stage unusual sights before a nation which is accustomed to turn to ridicule all that is not traditional."

The contrast between the two dramatic traditions struck Voltaire forcibly. English plays, no matter what other qualities they might have, were really dramatic. French plays, unless they were written with genius, were so hedged in by the thousand "don'ts" of the classical tradition that they were rather conversations about a series of events than a portrayal of the events themselves. Conservative and conventional in their taste, the French made exquisite fun of any attempt to bring about a change. They preferred the polished superficiality of a hackneyed subject, and formalized expression of emotion to the disturbing vitality of creative drama. Any attempt to give life and vigor to the dramatic formula of Corneille or Racine, now worn out, was damned at once by the universal decision that it was "not in good taste." The adoption of good taste as the supreme literary and dramatic standard allowed the French to condemn arbitrarily any movement that seemed likely to disturb their formal and polished existence. They enforced their decisions by the use of those two most effective weapons, irony and ridicule. Voltaire's contemporaries desired a tragic style that would keep its distance, something detached, conventional, and gracefully subdued. The theatre was an ornamental background in their artificial lives. If a play attempted to quit its allotted position in the background and to force itself into the inner consciousness of the audience, they became impatient and indignant. In the passage just quoted we have an almost unique example of Voltaire in energetic revolt against this complacent tradition.

Continuing, Voltaire compares Otway's play, *Venice Preserved*, with the French *Manlius*, of de la Fosse, based upon the same subject. He shows how the fastidious delicacy of the French robs their plays of those most necessary qualities, vitality and convincingness. After demonstrating the superiority of English vigor to French delicacy, he comes at length to what must have seemed to the French a most revolutionary position. He is rash enough to translate a scene from Shakespeare which is typical of all that the French considered to be barbaric and in bad taste — and to this scene (despite the fact that he deems the play as a whole to be filled with " barbaric irregularities ") Voltaire gives his unqualified approval. " In London with what pleasure I witnessed the tragedy, *Julius Caesar*, which has been the delight of your nation for a hundred and fifty years! Of course I cannot pretend to approve of the barbaric irregularities with which it abounds. It is only astonishing that there are not more of them in a work composed in an ignorant age by a man who did not even understand Latin and who had no guide

[179]

but his own genius. But, in the midst of so many gross faults, what was my rapture when I saw Brutus, still holding in his hand a dagger stained with the blood of Caesar, call together the Roman people, and from the Rostrum address them as follows. . . . "

Then Voltaire proceeds to give an accurate literal translation of Brutus' famous speech in the Forum after Caesar's death.[6] Continuing, Voltaire says, " After this scene Antony comes to move to pity these same barbarians in whom Brutus has instilled his rigor and his barbarity. Antony, by an artful speech, insensibly leads back these haughty spirits and, when he sees that they are softened, he shows them the body of Caesar and, making use of the most pathetic similes, he excites them to tumult and revenge."

Going back to Greek tragedy, upon which the French tradition was based, Voltaire admits that, " the Greek tragedies, although superior to the English, erred often in mistaking horror for terror, and the disgusting and unbelievable for the tragic and the marvelous. Art was in its infancy at the time of Aeschylus, as it was in London at the time of Shakespeare. But among the great faults of the Greek poets, and of yours too, one finds truly moving scenes and singular beauties."

Introducing a note of direct criticism, Voltaire says: " If certain Frenchmen, whose only knowledge of foreign tragedies and of foreign manners and customs are obtained through translations and hearsay, condemn them without qualification, they are, it seems to me, like blind

---

[6] It should be noted in passing that this is the only occasion on which Voltaire ever made an accurate and literal translation of Shakespeare.

men, who feel sure that a rose cannot be bright in color because they know only of its thorns. But if the Greeks and you have gone beyond the bounds of decency, and if the English especially have given frightful plays in the attempt to portray terror, we French, as cautious as you are rash, stop short of our mark for fear that we may be carried away, and at times fall short of tragedy, fearing that we will pass its bounds.

"I am far from proposing that the stage become a slaughter-house, as it is in the plays of Shakespeare and his successors, who, lacking his genius, have imitated only his faults. But I dare think that there are certain situations which still seem disgusting and horrible to the French which, carefully, treated and portrayed with art, and, above all, relieved by the charm of beautiful verse, could give us unexpected pleasure.

"*'There is no serpent, nor odious beast*
Which, depicted with art, will not please the eye.'
(Boileau, *Art Poet.*, III, 1, 2.)

"At least let someone tell me why our heroes and heroines are permitted to kill themselves on the stage, yet they are not allowed to kill anyone else there. Is the stage less bloody because of the death of Atalide, who stabs herself for her lover, than it would be because of the murder of Caesar? And if the sight of Cato's son, shown dead before his father, is made the occasion of an admirable discourse by that old Roman; if that passage has been greatly applauded in Italy and in England by people who are the most ardent defenders of the French rules of decency; if the most delicate women were not shocked, why do the French not accustom themselves to such things? Is not human nature the same in all people?

" All of these laws, to avoid bloodshed on the stage, to avoid having more than three people take part in a conversation, etc., are laws to which, it seems to me, we might take exception as did the ancient Greeks. There is a difference between the rules of decency, which are always somewhat arbitrary, and the fundamental laws of the theatre, the three unities."

These quotations give us an excellent idea of Voltaire's first attitude toward Shakespeare. There can be no doubt that, while he was in London, he was deeply moved by Shakespeare's art. No superficial realization of ordinary dramatic ability in the plays of the great English playwright would have caused Voltaire to attempt to change the course of the French dramatic tradition. Nevertheless, struck as he had been by the genius and by the originality of Shakespeare, when Voltaire returned to his native land he was quickly freed from any lingering doubts which he might have entertained as to the fundamental superiority of the classical system of tragedy. He was sincerely convinced that the established convention must remain the basis of French tragedy. Yet he desired to make use of the dramatic effects which he had so recently discovered. The conflict between these two viewpoints is the dominating influence in all of his early remarks about Shakespeare.

He had received a serious shock when La Motte Houdard, a talented dramatist with the prestige of membership in the French Academy behind him, came out in favor of the abolition of the unities, and suggested that tragedy should be written in prose. Answering La Motte's sacrilegious suggestions in the preface to the 1730 edition of *Oedipe*, Voltaire defended the unities with the greatest vehemence. He claimed that his attachment to the unities was because they were good and necessary, not because they were ancient, and he stated that he wished to overcome M. de la Motte by force of reason, not by authority. None the less, time and again Voltaire's argument in favor of the unities fell back on the fact that the ancient writers produced great plays by the use of that system, and consequently he felt that contemporary writers should use it.

Thus Voltaire's introduction of Shakespeare into France was always qualified by his concern for the unities. He feared that if he succeeded in making Shakespeare too popular in France, the latter's influence would become uncontrollable, and that the French would condone, if, indeed, they did not imitate, those "irregularities" which Voltaire so deplored. Consequently, while he brought Shakespeare's genius to the attention of his readers, he sought to keep before their eyes the fact that Shakespeare's lack of conformity to the rules detracted greatly from the beauty of his plays. When that had been made clear, he allowed a realization of the magnitude of Shakespeare's genius to be seen — and at these times he showed also, by implication, the futility of attempting to confine such genius within the limits of the French classical tradition.

The references to Shakespeare which were inserted in the *Essai sur la poésie épique*, when it was published in France in 1733, give an excellent example of Voltaire's manner of safeguarding his appreciation of Shakespeare. In the course of his remarks upon Homer he was attempting to explain the great popularity which the Greek poet had enjoyed in spite of his faults. He had long been puzzled by, the phenomenon. At last he found its parallel in Shakespeare. Shakespeare, too, had great faults, yet, according to Voltaire, his popularity was unrivaled in England.[7] The English thought him their greatest tragic poet, and almost invariably coupled with his name the epithet " divine." The announcement that one of his plays was to be acted was sufficient to fill the theatre, which could not be done by the *Cato* of Addison or the *Andromaque* of Racine, admirably translated as was the latter. Yet, he continues, these plays are monstrous. The plots of some of them cover many years; the hero is baptized in the first act and dies of old age in the last. He enumerates the various kinds of low and disgusting characters with which he considers Shakespeare's plays to be filled. " Picture," says Voltaire, " the most monstrous and most absurd things that you can. You will find them in Shakespeare. When I began to learn the English language I could not understand how so enlightened a people could admire an author so extravagant. But when I gained a fuller knowledge of the language, I perceived that the English were right, and that it is impossible for a whole nation to be deceived in a matter of sentiment, and to be wrong in being pleased. They saw, as I did, the gross faults of their favorite author, but they felt better than I his beauties, all the more remarkable because they are lightning flashes which have illuminated the most profound night. For a hundred and fifty years he has enjoyed his reputation.

---

[7] Here Voltaire was resorting to that favorite expedient of his, the distortion of facts to suit the needs of his argument. *Cf.* post, page 150.

Subsequent authors have served to increase, rather than to diminish it. The great intellect of the author of *Cato*, and that ability of his which made him a Secretary of State, could not enable him to place himself beside Shakespeare. Such is the privilege of creative genius. It strikes out for itself a path which no one has travelled before. It moves forward without guide, without art, without rule. It loses its way in its progress; but it leaves far behind it all which can boast only reason and correctness."

Voltaire's first thought was for the sacred unities; his greatest concern was, not to make Shakespeare popular, but to keep the influence of the great Englishman from becoming too widespread. As long as he felt that people restricted their appreciation of Shakespeare to those qualities of which he approved, Voltaire was pleased. He liked to think of the service which he had performed in bringing Shakespeare to the attention of the French. But as soon as the influence of Shakespeare had gone beyond the bounds which he had set, Voltaire did his utmost to stem the tide.

Because in his later life Voltaire showed the most violent opposition to Shakespeare, it has been supposed that his attitude underwent a distinct change from what it had been on his return from England. Often it has been taken for granted that, as he became older, Voltaire became jealous of Shakespeare's increasing prestige and sought by his criticism to detract from it. This supposition would account for the contrast between the keen appreciation that he showed at the time we are discussing and the bitterness of his attacks on Shakespeare in later life. But such a theory does not account for Voltaire's apparently contradictory views concerning the great Elizabethan in the very first passages in which he mentions him, the *Essai sur la poésie épique*, and the *Discours sur la tragédie*. Voltaire's attitude toward Shakespeare did not change; the attitude of his contemporaries did change, radically. In the various remarks about Shakespeare which he made soon after his return from England, Voltaire felt that he had assumed the most liberal attitude compatible with any respect for the classical tradition. And even at this time he emphasized Shakespeare's faults quite as much as his virtues. Consequently, when, as a result of his own evangelical work, Voltaire saw French popular opinion becoming too unrestricted in its appreciation of the great English dramatist, he considered himself free to oppose the growing Shakespearian cult without feeling the slightest inconsistency in his attitude.

The letter on *Tragédie* in the *Lettres Philosophiques* contains much less of Shakespeare and much more of Voltaire than his other accounts of the English writer. Prefacing his remarks with a concise summary of Shakespeare's historical position in English drama, Voltaire says: " The English as well as the Spaniards possessed an organized theatre at a time when the French were entertained by mere mountebanks. Shakespeare, who was considered the Corneille of England, flourished at about the same time as Lope de Vega. He created the theatre. He had a fertile genius, powerful, unaffected, and sublime, without the slightest spark of good taste or the slightest knowledge of dramatic rules. . . . I am going to venture a bold statement, yet it is true. The very talents of that author have caused the downfall of the English stage. Such beautiful scenes, such majestic, such terrifying fragments are scattered through these monstrous farces which go by the name of tragedy that they have always been performed with great success. Time, which alone assures the reputation of men, ends by making their failings respectable. Most of the bizarre and grotesque ideas of this writer have acquired, after two hundred years, the right to be considered sublime. Almost all modern writers have copied them; but where Shakespeare succeeded, they are hissed, and you may well believe that the veneration in which this ancient writer is held increases in proportion to the disdain with which modern writers are looked upon. They do not realize that he should not be imitated. The lack of success which his copyists meet only makes people think that he is inimitable."

After instances taken from *Othello* and *Hamlet* of the monstrosities that may be found in Shakespeare, Voltaire gives an example of the manner in which his successors imitated the great Elizabethan. His choice of Otway's play, *Venice Preserved,* as an example is significant. In the *Discours sur la tragédie* he had given a long and detailed comparison of this very play and the *Manlius* of de la Fosse. In this first essay, as we have seen, he used Otway's play to show the advantages of the lack of restriction placed upon English dramatists, and he had commented upon the fact that *Venice Preserved,* with its dramatic tenseness, its directness, its simplicity, was a much better play than the French one on the same subject. And he had given as a reason for the superiority of the English play the fact that the French author had been so handicapped by the French dramatic rules that he had been unable to produce a good play. Here in the *Lettres Philosophiques* he chose the same example that he had used in his former essay. One who is acquainted with the manner in which each sentence, each word in the *Lettres Philosophiques* were carefully selected to obtain a definite effect cannot fail to realize that the choice of Otway's play was a deliberate attempt by Voltaire to offset his former remarks.

In his former essay he had translated into French a passage in which Shakespeare had violated many of the rules of decency. He had depicted a corpse and a bloody dagger upon the stage, he had introduced a boisterous, unruly mob before the spectators, and, worst of all, he had caused successive orators to arouse the passions of this mob. Without doubt Voltaire had many qualms of conscience for the unqualified approval which he had given this scene. He was determined not to be so rash again, yet he desired to translate another scene from the English dramatist. " No doubt," he says, " you complain that up to this time those who have told you about the English theatre, and especially about this famous Shakespeare, have only exposed his errors to you, and that no one has translated one of those striking passages which force one to pardon all his faults. In answer I would say that it is very easy to translate into prose the errors of a poet, but it is most difficult to translate his beautiful verses. Those scribblers who set themselves up as critics of famous writers, compose masses of books. I would prefer to those tomes two pages that introduce us to new beauties, for I have always held, as have all men of good taste, that a dozen verses of Homer or of Virgil are more worth while than all the criticisms that have been made of these two great men. I have ventured to translate fragments from the best English poets; the following is from Shakespeare. Forgive the copy on behalf of the original, and when you see a translation always remember that you see only a feeble engraving of a beautiful picture.

"I have chosen the soliloquy from the tragedy, *Hamlet*, which everyone knows, and which starts with the verse:

"'*To be or not to be, that is the question.*'

"Hamlet, prince of Denmark, speaks . . . ."

Nothing is more significant of Voltaire's changed attitude than the difference between his former translation of Brutus' famous speech and this translation from *Hamlet*. Re-translated into English, Voltaire's transcription of Shakespeare reads as follows:

"'*Hold, it is necessary to choose and to pass at once*
From life to death, from existence to nothingness.
Cruel gods, if there be any gods, enlighten my heart.
Must I grow old, bowed under the hand that insults me?
Must I endure, or may I end my ill-fortune and my fate?
Who am I? What holds me back? And what is death?
It is the end of all my ills, it is my sole refuge.
After long delirium it is a peaceful sleep.
One falls asleep and everything dies. But a ghastly awakening
May perhaps succeed the pleasures of sleep.

We are threatened; we are told that this short life
Is immediately followed by eternal torments.
O death! fatal moment! dreadful eternity!
Every heart at thy mere name is congealed with terror.
Ah! Who could, without thee, endure this life?
Who could bless the hypocrisy of our lying priests?
Flatter the faults of an unworthy mistress?
Grovel under a minister of state, pay court to his
pride?
And show the weakness of his downcast soul
To ingrate friends, who turn away their eyes?
Death would be too sweet in extremities like these,
But doubt speaks, and cries to us: Stop.
It forbids our hands indulging in that happy homicide,
And of a warlike hero makes a timid Christian,[7a]

[7a] Voltaire's French is as follows:

   " Demeure; il faut choisir, et passer à l'instant
     De la vie à la mort, ou de l'être au néant.
     Dieux justes! s'il en est, éclairez mon courage.
     Faut-il vieillir courbé sous la main qui m'outrage,
     Supporter ou finir mon malheur et mon sort?
     Qui suis-je? qui m'arrête? et qu'est-ce que la mort?
     C'est la fin de nos maux, c'est mon unique asile;
     Après de longs transports, c'est un sommeil tranquille;
     On s'endort, et tout meurt. Mais un affreux réveil
     Doit succéder peut-être aux douceurs du sommeil.
     On nous menace, on dit que cette courte vie
     De tourments éternels est aussitôt suivie.
     O mort! moment fatal! affreuse éternité!
     Tout coeur à ton seul nom se glace, épouvanté.
     Eh! qui pourrait, sans toi, supporter cette vie,
     De nos prêtres menteurs bénir l'hypocrisie,
     D'une indigne maîtresse encenser les erreurs,
     Ramper sous un ministre, adorer ses hauteurs,
     Et montrer les langueurs de son âme abattue
     A des amis ingrats qui détournent la vue?

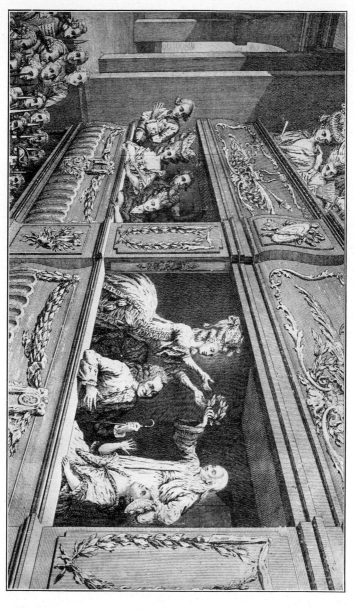

"Do not think that I have translated the English word for word. Woe unto those literal translators who, by translating each word, lose the sense of a passage. In such matters one can certainly say that the letter kills, while the spirit revives."

Frankly, what comment can one make upon such a travesty? The passage is an excellent example of Voltaire's literary ability, but that it should be given as representative of Shakespeare's genius! One is almost disappointed that Voltaire does not add the finishing touch and comment upon the similarity between his own style and Shakespeare's. A supplementary interest in the passage is the light it sheds on Voltaire's character and methods. He was persistent in introducing in every conceivable form and place his attacks upon political and religious institutions. Here it is Shakespeare whom he quotes as speaking of "the hypocrisy of our lying priests," and of "paying court to the pride of ministers of state." He had no scruples against inserting his own sentiments into supposed translations. It was by far the safest method of undermining those powerful corporations, the Church and the State. And Voltaire was confident that he was doing Shakespeare a favor when he included such material. He had already discovered that such statements as these added to the popularity of his own writings. He had no reason to doubt that they would perform the same service for Shakespeare.

La mort serait trop douce en ces extrémités;
Mais le scrupule parle, et nous crie: Arrêtez.
Il défend à nos mains cet heureux homicide,
Et d'un héros guerrier fait un chrétien timide, etc."

After reading this translation of Hamlet's soliloquy, one would feel justified in stating that Voltaire had not the slightest knowledge of the nature of Shakespeare's genius, and that he had utterly failed to understand the fundamental characteristics of English literature. Yet, just as we are coming to such conclusions, Voltaire ends this passage in the *Lettres Philosophiques* with such a striking simile that, in spite of ourselves, we are forced to admit his deep comprehension of the essential qualities of English literature. Seldom has a more acute summary of the English genius been made than this one by Voltaire: " Those brilliant and monstrous plays of Shakespeare are a thousand times more pleasing than our modern sophistication. Up to now, the poetic genius of the English has resembled a bushy tree planted by nature, throwing out at haphazard a thousand branches, and growing unsymmetrically, yet with vigor. If you tried to make it into something different and trimmed it like one of the trees in the Marly gardens, you would kill it." Thus did Voltaire characterize the difference between the conventional regularity of French literature and the extravagant originality which is typical of the literature of England.

In emphasizing Shakespeare's faults as a dramatist, Voltaire fortified the position that he had determined to take as a playwright. He had decided to introduce into his plays some of the qualities that seemed most striking to him in Shakespeare's work, and his criticisms both of Shakespeare and of the French dramatists were calculated to aid him in assuming this new position. When he criticized the French tradition he showed that the innovations upon which he had decided were needed in France; when he criticized Shakespeare's irregularity he prepared his audiences to find in his own work the qualities of Shakespeare's greatness without his weaknesses. Voltaire, already acknowledged to be one of the three greatest French dramatists, was not satisfied with his position. By combining in his own work the best to be found in the French and the English traditions, he had determined to place himself upon the solitary pedestal of dramatic supremacy. The only flaw in his plan was that he lacked the essential quality both of Shakespeare and of Corneille and Racine — dramatic genius. To a certain extent he mastered the technique, but he was unable to grasp the spirit that animated them.

Mr. Haines, in his excellent study of Shakespeare in France, has analyzed the influence of Shakespeare upon Voltaire's plays.[8] He has shown the debt of *Brutus* to *Julius Caesar*, of *Eriphyle* to *Hamlet*, of *Zaïre* to *Othello*. Voltaire himself claimed that the *Mort de César* was " after the English manner." *Adélaïde du Gueschlin* seemed so English to the French that Voltaire was accused of having produced " gory imitations of that stage butcher called Shakespeare." He had, indeed, caused a cannon to be fired on the stage and one of the characters to appear with his arm in a sling! Both *Sémiramis* and

[8] C. M. Haines, *Shakespeare in France, Criticism, Voltaire to Victor Hugo*, published by the Shakespeare Society, London, 1925. On this subject see also Jusserand, *Shakespeare in France*, London, 1899, and Lounsbury, *Shakespeare and Voltaire*, New York, 1902. The reader is also referred to these three books for a discussion of Voltaire's attitude toward Shakespeare in his later life. Interesting as these two subjects are, from considerations of space they must remain outside the scope of the present work.

Eriphyle are reminiscent of *Hamlet*. Voltaire, following Shakespeare, ventured to have a ghost appear upon the stage — a dangerous experiment when one remembers that the ghost was forced to make its way through the witty young fops whose seats lined the stage! An examination of Voltaire's plays shows that he was indulging very timorously the public taste for a romantic tinge to its drama, but it was a romantic tinge carefully cloaked in the classical form. As Mr. Lytton Strachey has said, " The wild diversity of his incidents shows a trend towards the romantic, which, doubtless, under happier influences, would have led him much further along the primrose path which ended in the bonfire of 1830." [9]

But, after all, our main interest in Voltaire's relation to Shakespeare is the discovery of what might have been, — the uncovering of the conflict between Voltaire, the theorist, who recognized the shortcomings of the French dramatic tradition and the vitality and genius of Shakespeare, and Voltaire, the practical dramatist, afraid to venture anything upon the stage for which he did not foresee popular approval.

If anything could have made Voltaire an independent dramatist the influence of the English stage would have done it. We have seen the doubts that were raised in his mind concerning the infallibility of the French theory of tragedy. We have seen also how readily he put aside his misgivings when he realized that his attempt to change the established tradition might imperil the sacred unities. Voltaire, who gained immortal fame by his refusal to ac-

[9] Strachey, *op. cit.*, p. 154.

cept the authority of convention and tradition in a thousand different ways, who was the great apostle of the rule of reason, who depended upon reason to solve all problems, this analytical, logical Voltaire discarded logic when the drama was in question. It is significant that his present reputation depends solely upon his achievements in those realms of thought in which he refused to accept the authority of tradition and custom.

In one sense, Shakespeare's actual influence upon Voltaire was negligible. No amount of influence could have made Voltaire a good dramatist; no model, no matter how carefully followed, could have changed the essential qualities of his plays. A play, to be of more than passing interest must possess one of two qualities. It must have in it either convincing characterization and dialogue, or else decided dramatic tenseness. Voltaire's knowledge of people was too superficial to allow him to give the breath of life to the characters in his plays. His sense of the dramatic was too slight to give his plays true excitement of plot. As a result his plays are, to us, both lifeless and dull.

If, we ask, Voltaire possessed none of the qualities essential to a dramatist, how did it happen that his plays were unrivaled in their popularity for more than half a century? The answer is that in place of the true dramatic gift Voltaire possessed to a superlative degree that ability to sense the desires and reactions of his contemporaries which, in our present age, is possessed to a certain extent by an editor, a theatrical producer, an advertising man, or any other person who is dependent for his livelihood upon analyzing or sensing the desires of the public. But Vol-

taire exploited popular feelings instinctively, not with pre-
meditation. Popularity and success were life blood in his
veins. Without them he could not exist. The slightest
hint that he did not possess popular confidence was likely
to send him into a frenzy. The most insignificant attack
by, a petty scribbler made him uneasy, and caused him to
open up the powerful batteries of his satire in his own defense. So far was this desire for popularity characteristic of Voltaire that a prominent French historian, after a
careful examination of all of Voltaire's works, has come
to the conclusion that each of them was written merely
to meet a popular desire for such a book. Such a conclusion
is, of course, exaggerated, but in its essence it is just. Voltaire was unable to write a book for which he did not
expect popularity. And seldom was he deceived. When
Voltaire spoke, Europe listened attentively and applauded
almost without pausing to determine the meaning of his
words.

Aided by his masterful dramatic technique, Voltaire
filled the void caused by his lack of genuine dramatic ability by introducing into his plays matters of local and contemporary interest. Instead of achieving by dramatic
means the suspense which a play requires, he stirred up
momentary interest and excitement by reference to ideas
and movements which were intensely interesting because
of their relation to the sentiments of the time. He voiced
the ideas of his contemporaries, and in so doing aroused
their enthusiasm for his plays. They, mistakenly, believed
their interest to be due to legitimate dramatic effects. And,
of course, poor dramatist that he was, Voltaire was greatly
superior to the other French eighteenth century play-

wrights. In its choice of plays the eighteenth century was restricted to the mediocre contemporary productions or the masterpieces of a by-gone age. That it gave a warm reception to the best of its own dramatic attempts is easily understood.

CHAPTER ELEVEN
COSMOPOLITANISM

CHAPTER ELEVEN

COSMOPOLITANISM

THE most superficial examination of the cosmopolitan movement shows to what an amazing extent the instinct to revolt against conventional standards may dominate a period. It would seem that the history of thought and of literature is merely the chronicle of a succession of reactions against accepted standards. Certainly in France the eighteenth century differed from its predecessor as widely as was possible. The subjects in which the eighteenth century was interested, its literary style, its ambitions, its methods, its ethics, were diametrically opposed to those of the *Grand Siècle*. Two great figures in French history, Bossuet and Voltaire, typify their respective centuries. Bossuet, profound, dignified, serious, and puritanical, placed his faith in the authority of tradition; Voltaire, superficial, undignified, gay, and liberal, attacked tradition in his battle for the supremacy of reason. The more one compares their characters, the more marked is the contrast. Bossuet condemned the arts because they aroused passions; Voltaire himself strove to stir up these passions. Voltaire's life was spent in attacking; Bossuet's in defending. Voltaire continually sought praise and public approval; Bossuet, sure of himself, disdained them both. Voltaire revolted against all that Bossuet had stood for, and the eighteenth century joined him in this revolution.

Eighteenth century writers felt limited and confined by the past. The old tradition smothered their wit and spontaneity with its cynical impersonality, its order, its restraint, and its erudition. The intellectual communion of Paris, Rome, and Athens did not appeal to the new generation; young writers were interested in their own personalities and in the people around them, not in intellectual theories. With impetuous recklessness they discarded tradition, and determined to do without the accumulated experience of France's long centuries of civilization. The century was, as M. Faguet said, " entirely new, primitive, and, as one might say, unhewn. Tradition is the experience of a nation; it lacked tradition, and would have none of it." [1] It had the impetuous, exuberant inexperience of youth.

Nowhere is the revolt more strikingly brought out than in the attitude of the eighteenth century toward England. Under Louis XIV, as we have seen, the French had looked upon England as a barren and barbarous island; in its reaction against the classical tradition, the eighteenth century went to England for its greatest inspirations. The Huguenot exiles brought to the attention of Frenchmen the real worth of English literature and the fundamental solidity of English thought. By personal investigation various French writers came to share the enthusiasm of the Huguenots, and succeeded in imparting it to the nation as a whole. There followed a period of intense Anglomania. So far did French enthusiasm for English literature go that in 1753 Voltaire, who had been one of the most ardent supporters of the English, became

[1] Faguet, *Dix-huitième Siècle*, p. xii.

disgusted at the unwarranted popularity of mediocre English books, and observed that, " the booksellers (who are always in style) sell novels under the label ' English ' in the same way that people sell English ribbons and lace." Gibbon, who visited Paris in 1763, wrote, " Our opinions, our manners, even our dress were adopted in France." [2] From having been so critical of the English that they were unable to appreciate them at all, the French had become so indiscriminate in their enthusiasm that they could not choose between the good and the bad in England. But this interest was more than a desire to make up for their former ignorance; it was more than a desire to contradict the judgment of the seventeenth century. The French found in the English scientific method the stimulus that was to replace that which they lost when they abandoned the classical tradition.

Along with the other theories of the *Grand Siècle*, the eighteenth century abandoned the positive manner in which Descartes had put forth his speculations, which had heretofore been the standard of scientific and logical thought. In its place it adopted the less fallible experimental method of Bacon and Newton. This experimental method it applied to the problem of life, and thereby established a new branch of thought — political science.

The eighteenth century has been advertised as an age of philosophers, but, as far as abstract metaphysics and theology are concerned, never was a period less philosophical. The eighteenth century discovered the world we live in. It sought to determine the universal facts of life. It is doubtless because it was not scientific and erudite,

[2] Texte, *op. cit.*, p. 78.

but light, and intensely human, that the eighteenth century is so fascinating, and that its influence upon posterity has been so marked. Just as Newton first collected all possible evidence upon the manner in which the laws of nature operate, and afterward formulated his theories, so eighteenth century "philosophers" sought to determine the universal characteristics of man in order to raise above mere conjecture their generalizations about him. Inspired by the scientific spirit, they observed human nature and examined the findings of human experience, that they might have broad premises upon which to base their conclusions, instead of being forced to rely upon intuition and intellectual speculation. It was obvious that to collect the information they desired, they would have to include the entire world in their investigation. It was the pursuit of this universal investigation that led to cosmopolitanism.

The eighteenth century investigators were intensely practical. To them all theories not based on human experience were valueless, and all speculation that had not as its end the betterment of man's estate was useless. They were realists and optimists. Their excitement over the new discovery made them expect from it everything that man could desire. Confident in their new methods, they wanted to overthrow all such arbitrary and restrictive institutions as dogmatic religion and patriotism. Optimism was their religion and the world their fatherland. To be citizens of the world was their ambition. They, sought the universal. The success of Newton's scientific method had demonstrated the universality of the laws of nature. These "philosophers" were convinced that human nature, too, was universal, and that national boundaries were useless.

They admired and tried to comprehend those things that were most foreign to their natures, for in so doing they hoped to arrive at a universal understanding of the world. The cosmopolitan spirit was responsible for most of the significant movements in the eighteenth century: for its weakness as well as its strength, for its breadth of knowledge and its shallowness, its incisive understanding and its superficiality, for the popular acceptance of its theories and for their mistaken premises, for its deism, its lack of patriotism, its wit, its realism, its altruism. The whole seething, hysterical, romantic, scientific exuberance of the eighteenth century was a result of the acceptance of this new point of view.

When historians recount the development of thought in any period, the necessity for clarity forces them to omit insignificant detail, to organize their material, until it would seem that a master mind had arranged for the development of the period, and that the individuals of any movement merely, fit themselves into a pre-arranged schedule. In practice human development is never as orderly as that. Seldom do men see clearly the direction in which they and their contemporaries are working. The eighteenth century was conscious of no organized plan for the development of the cosmopolitan spirit. There was, instead, in prominent individuals at that time a widespread desire to break down the restrictive barriers of the seventeenth century, and to explore the world. That instinct led Montesquieu to make the famous tour of Europe in which he collected the data upon comparative government that he included in the *Esprit des Lois* — in its conception one of the most cosmopolitan books ever published.

The same desire caused most prominent Frenchmen to visit England during the first half of the eighteenth century. It was a desire to codify the information collected as a result of these explorations that led to the encyclopedic movement. The tendency of eighteenth century writers to stress the cosmopolitan spirit was in large part their reaction against the classical tradition in France.

This inquiring state of mind, this desire to abandon the intellectual limits set by the classical tradition and to explore the world of thought, was at its height when Voltaire was in England. Voltaire exploited it. Where it had been vague and nebulous, he gave it concrete foundation and objective; he consolidated and concentrated it.

Struck as he was by the fallacies and injustices of the French system, convinced by what he saw in England that it would be possible to have a better order without sacrificing those features he considered essential in government, Voltaire left England prepared to do his utmost to change conditions in France. He sought to bring home to his compatriots the striking contrast he had felt in England. He wrote the *Lettres Philosophiques* to show the French the advantages of English liberty and tolerance. The subject of the *Histoire de Charles XII* gave him a chance to examine social conditions in various parts of Europe and to point out in passing the advantages and defects of the different systems. Both of these works, as well as *Brutus* and the *Essai sur la poésie épique*, were written with definite forethought as to their effect upon the French. No Frenchman reading them could miss the contrast between his own and other governments. Until now the French had ignored what went on in other lands; there had been little chance to compare their own conditions with those of other people, and accordingly they had been satisfied. By means of widespread comparison, Voltaire showed them that not only was French society not the only form possible, but that it did not even rank very high (as far as personal liberty was concerned) when compared to other European countries. Voltaire left England determined to break down the indifferent contentment of his fellow-countrymen, and his weapon was this conception of cosmopolitanism.

In large part he inaugurated this campaign in three books, the *Essay on Epick Poetry*, the *Histoire de Charles XII*, and the *Lettres Philosophiques*. To understand his aims, it is necessary to examine these works.

The *Essay on Epick Poetry* was Voltaire's first public expression of the cosmopolitan spirit, and, despite its advertising purpose, it is in some ways more unprejudiced and universal than any of his works. The subject of the essay, the comparative merits of various national epics, required impartiality and freedom from national prejudice. One wonders whether it was not during the preparation of this work that Voltaire first saw the advantages in universal comparison, and in the appreciation of the literature of all nations. It may be in some part due to the fact that he was writing for an English audience that we find more tolerance and less national egoism and bias in this treatise than in almost any of Voltaire's other works.

In his introduction to this essay Voltaire gives in one sentence the fundamental reason for cosmopolitanism.

" What belongs to good Sense, belongs to all Nations of the World." [3] This attempt to broaden the sympathy of all countries, and to allow nations to appreciate each other's masterpieces, absorbed much of Voltaire's attention. Today we are prone to discount the importance of such a point of view as this, because it is universally accepted. We willingly acknowledge that Voltaire is " modern " in spirit, but it is hard to think that statements of this nature, which to us are axiomatic and banal, were once highly original, even revolutionary.

In this essay Voltaire was ostensibly attempting to fix the limits of epic poetry. In reality he was doing something far more significant. He was analyzing and attempting to discount national prejudice. He was attempting to discover what did belong to " good sense." He was differentiating between national and universal appreciation. " The Point of the Question," he says, " and of the Difficulty, is to know what all polite Nations agree upon, and in what they differ." [4] He goes on to say, " There are Beauties which the Taste of every Nation equally relish. . . . But still our particular Customs have introduc'd among them all, a new Sort of Taste, peculiar to each Nation. . . . From their different Characters flows that dislike which every Nation shows for the Taste of its Neighbour." [5] After giving examples of different national tastes, Voltaire states his formula for cosmopolitan appreciation: " He [the judicious reader] will mark the Progresses, the Sinking of the Art, its Rising again, and pursue it through its various Changes. He will distinguish the Beauties, and the Faults that are such, everywhere, and in all Ages,

---

[3] White, *op. cit.*, p. 83.   [4] *Id.*, p. 83.   [5] *Id.*, p. 85.

from those doubtful Things which are call'd Blemishes by one Nation, and still'd Perfections by another." [6]

Later on Voltaire gives a concrete example of the possible benefits of such appreciation. " Would each Nation attend a little more than they do, to the Taste and the Manners of their respective Neighbours, perhaps a general good Taste might diffuse itself through all *Europe* from such an intercourse of Learning, and from that useful Exchange of Observations. The *English* Stage, for Example, might be clear'd of mangled Carcasses, and the style of their tragic Authors, come down from their forced Metaphorical Bombast to a nearer Imitation of Nature. The *French* would learn from the *English* to animate their Tragedies with more Action, and would contract, now and then, their long Speeches into shorter and warmer Sentiments." [7]

Voltaire was intent upon making people think for themselves; he wanted them to apply their powers of reasoning to every subject. He sought to enlarge the material for an examination of human experience, and to take up every question anew and from an unprejudiced standpoint. " Our just respect for the Ancients," he says, " proves a mere Superstition, if it betrays us into a rash Contempt for our Neighbours and Countrymen. We ought not to do such an Injury to Nature, as to shut our eyes to all the Beauties that her Hands pour around us, in order to look back fixedly upon her former Productions." [8]

These few quotations give an idea of the extent to which Voltaire had become imbued with the cosmopolitan

[6] *Id.*, p. 88. 　　　 [7] *Id.*, p. 135. 　　　 [8] *Id.*, p. 87.

spirit. It is significant that in his first book after his departure from France he should express himself in this manner, for cosmopolitanism was the most important influence of England upon Voltaire, and it was the one influence that was undoubtedly due to England alone. Voltaire might possibly have encountered the various other influences of England had he remained in France, but had it not been for the vivid contrast of the two countries that he saw with his own eyes at this time, he would never have realized the many valuable qualities that nations neglected in each other because of national prejudice and convention. The liberal tradition of England had given him a wider horizon and more universal interests.

The *Essay on Epick Poetry* is of interest primarily because it is the first of Voltaire's books to give voice to his growing conviction that in the cosmopolitan spirit is to be found the most rational attitude toward life and literature. This short essay did not have any great influence upon the people who read it. Far different were the two other books that came as direct results of his experience in England. Both the *Histoire de Charles XII* and the *Lettres Philosophiques* had a profound effect upon the eighteenth century and upon modern history.

The *Histoire de Charles XII* was a new kind of history. It was universal in interest, and it was impartial. In it Voltaire did not attempt to prove any theory; he was interested neither in glorifying nor in defaming any person or any country. To the best of his ability, he stated impartially the available facts; he examined all sides of a disputed point and submitted all of his material to the laws of evidence and of psychology. Voltaire is generally admitted to have re-discovered the comparative method in modern history. This book is the first example of the use of that method since the Greek historians.

That Voltaire, the poet, the wit, the society man, should suddenly produce a serious history, is in itself extraordinary. There had been no warning that he would do anything of the sort. It was startling that in this history he should evolve an historical method that was destined soon to be in universal use. What caused him to do it? What turned his attention to such an unusual subject as the history of a Swedish king? It was his desire to make known the cosmopolitan spirit. We have already noted the manner in which he collected material for this book. His reason for writing it was the opportunity such a subject gave him for a further exposition of the cosmopolitan spirit. The *Histoire de Charles XII* shows the increased grasp of Voltaire's mind as a result of his exile in England. Formerly he had been limited by the boundaries of France; now his interest takes in all of the civilized world.

The *Histoire de Charles XII* gives a much surer opportunity of judging Voltaire's development in England, and of appreciating his knowledge of European conditions, both social, political, and religious, than does the *Lettres Philosophiques*. The latter was written with the express purpose of criticizing, if not of reforming, France. It is inaccurate and biased; polemical, rather than historical. In his history of the Swedish king, Voltaire is not attempting to attack or to defend; he is writing impartially, and it is in this book that we find his attitude summed up most accurately.

Voltaire is often presented to us as a lank, nervous,

less do people dare present petitions against crown ministers, for the Sultan ordinarily turns such things over to
the ministers concerned without reading them." [11]

It is, however, chiefly in the realm of politics and religion
that Voltaire stirred up the French by a contrast of conditions. In many, ways he brought to light the advantages
and the failings of hereditary aristocracy. He realized the
essential uselessness and lack of occupation of the nobility
in France, and he compared conditions there to those in
other countries. He preferred the English system where
the nobles took an essential part in the activities of the
country. But at the same time he brought to the attention
of the French the possibility of a system in which there
was no hereditary aristocracy. Such a passage as the following came as a surprise to many French readers, to
whom hereditary nobility seemed the only feasible form
of government.

" The Grand Vizier . . . was the son of a peasant
from the village of Chourlou. Such parentage is nothing to
be ashamed of among the Turks. They have no nobility.
They, have neither hereditary posts, requiring definite
duties, nor family titles; service alone is supposed to account for all advance. This is the custom in almost all
the orient. *A very natural and very good custom* if the
offices would be distributed only upon merit; but the
Viziers are usually only the dependants of a black eunuch,
or of a favorite slave." [12]

Here Voltaire is not trying to force an opinion upon his
readers; he is attempting to make them realize the essen-

[11] *Id.*, p. 223.
[12] *Id.*, p. 220. The italics are the author's.

[214]

CHARLES XII, KING OF SWEDEN

tial problems of government. He shows them the theoretical advantages of a democratic form of government, but at the same time he points out the usual failure of such a government to function properly.

When he discusses Poland, Voltaire investigates another theory of government. He shows his readers the defects and the advantages of a government in which the supreme power is in the hands of an armed nobility.

" The nobles, who make the laws of the republic, make up its armed force. On great occasions they mount their horses, and constitute a body of more than a hundred thousand men. This great army, called Pospolite, moves with difficulty, and governs itself badly. The difficulty in obtaining food and forage makes it impossible for it to remain assembled for any great length of time. It lacks discipline, subordination, and experience, but the love of liberty with which it is animated makes it always formidable. . . . Each gentleman has a vote in the election of a king, and may himself be chosen to that office. With this most cherished privilege is connected one of the greatest of abuses. The throne is almost always up for auction, and, as a Pole is rarely rich enough to buy it, it has often been sold to foreigners. The nobles and the clergy defend against their king the liberty which they steal from the rest of the nation. The common people are slaves. Such is the destiny of man that, by one means or another, the majority is always subjugated by the minority! The peasant does not sow for himself, but for the lords, to whom he belongs, as do his fields and his labor; and these lords can sell him, or butcher him, as they do the beasts of the fields. . . . The nobility, jealous of its liberty, often sells its votes, but seldom its affections. Scarcely have they elected a king when they begin to fear his ambition, and commence intrigues against him. The men whom he has made great, and whom he may not remove, often become his enemies, instead of remaining his retainers. Those nobles who remain attached to the court are the object of the hatred of the rest of the nobility. This causes the perpetual existence of two parties, an inevitable, even a necessary division in a country where people wish to have a king, and yet to retain their liberty." [13]

In another passage Voltaire takes up some of the things that are indispensable to a good ruler. He shows that the Sultan of Turkey, too haughty to send ambassadors to foreign courts, was in deep ignorance of what went on between other nations, and, indeed, of what was happening in his own country. "The Sultan," he says, "shut off in his harem among women and eunuchs, sees only through the eyes of his Grand Vizier. This minister, as inaccesible as his master, busy with petty intrigues of the harem and out of contact with the world outside, is either himself deceived, or else he deceives the Sultan." [14]

The picture that Voltaire draws of the injustice and the confusion resulting from the Sultan's lack of contact with his subjects resembles strikingly the accounts that are given us of conditions fifty years later at Versailles, where the French king, weakly bowing to the wishes of the women of his court, knew little more of the conditions in his kingdom than did the Sultan. What would Voltaire, intent upon driving home the dangers of such a condition, not have given to be able to quote the famous sentence

[13] *Id.*, p. 85 ff.   [14] *Id.*, p. 269.

which Marie Antoinette was to speak, " What! They have no bread? Why don't they eat cake? "

Continuing his lesson in political science, Voltaire discusses war. In a short passage in which he points out the disasters which were in store for Poland, whether she were successful or defeated in the projected war, he shows in reality, the almost invariable futility of taking up arms. " The Poles knew that if this war . . . turned out disastrously for them, their country, defenceless on all sides, would be the prey of the Swedish king; and that if it were successful, they would be subjugated by their own king, who, master of Livonia and Saxony, would enslave Poland between these two countries."

In a passage in which he compares Charles XII and Peter the Great, Voltaire gives a most penetrating estimate of the permanent values of two contrasting policies. He sums up the two kings as they appeared before the memorable battle of Pultava. " Charles, famous because of his nine years of victories; Peter, because of nine years spent in an attempt to make his soldiers equal to those of the Swedish king; the one glorious because he had founded new states, the other for having civilized his own; Charles had the title " Invincible " which might be snatched from him in a single instant; the world at large had already bestowed the title " Great " upon Peter, and no defeat could wrest it from him, for he owed it to no victory." [15]

Voltaire is commonly supposed to have preferred a benevolent despotism to any other form of government, but a passage in which he sums up the influence of Charles

[15] *Id.*, p. 196.

XII shows that he realized the grave dangers to be encountered if unrestricted power is to be placed in the hands of one man. After showing that Charles, were he to reestablish his position following his return from Turkey, had it in his power to disrupt the peace of every country in Europe and to cause untold misery and suffering, Voltaire remarks: " So dangerous may one man become when he has unrestricted power in a great country, and is endowed with breadth of spirit and courage." [16]

Such passages as these made the *Histoire de Charles XII* a real education in comparative government. Voltaire had little need actually to point out the differences between the governments that he described and the French system. He showed the French how other countries were governed. To each country that he discussed he applied the cool analytic methods of modern historical criticism; he explained the manner in which each government was supposed to function according to the theory upon which it was based, and he showed where each theory failed in actual practice. Voltaire's French readers unconsciously applied this method of criticism to their own country, and, almost without realizing it, found themselves becoming dissatisfied.

The *Histoire de Charles XII* does not show the full development of Voltaire's historical theories. They were not expressed in their complete form until the publication of the *Essai sur les Moeurs*. In his history of the Swedish king his desire to show the hopelessness, the futility of war has caused him to pay more attention to wars and to the campaigns of various generals than in his other his-

[16] *Id.*, p. 363.

tories. The nature of the men with whom he was dealing caused him to emphasize the personalities of kings and of prominent men as he did not in his later works. Despite these weaknesses, however, the *Histoire de Charles XII* stands forth clearly as the first modern history.

At last, Voltaire's essential political opinions had become fixed. He believed the problem of government to be a science, and that like other sciences it should be based upon the laws of reason, upon the observation of the realities of life, upon the experience of the human race. History, properly told, is the exposition of human experience, and for that reason Voltaire became interested in history and in historical methods.

The *Historie de Charles XII* is especially important because of the light it sheds upon Voltaire's knowledge at this period of the principles of politics and government. It has been generally supposed that he failed to understand the basic principles of the English political system. This accusation has been brought against him because in the *Lettres Philosophiques,* the book in which he pretends to expose to our eyes his reactions toward England, he does not mention the method by which the English acquired that liberty which he so greatly envied. It has been taken for granted that he was still the shallow, superficial poet that he was when he left France.

In England political freedom started in the small unit of the town or manor. The people themselves built up and maintained a tradition of liberty, gradually increasing the size of the units in which they were able to exercise it. When the movement finally became widespread, historians and philosophers theorized about it. Subsequent history has shown that French liberty came as a result of the popularization of the theories of government. Contrary to the manner of the English, the French started with theories of right and liberty, and by a process of vulgarization obtained physical possession of the privileges they coveted. The process was in strict keeping with their fundamentally logical nature. In the *Lettres Philosophiques* Voltaire started one of the most important of the movements that brought about the full possession of political liberty by the French. In this work he did not mention the manner in which the English had obtained their liberty. The reason for this method of attack is that he fully understood the character of the French. He knew that they would obtain the desired end in another way, and in this work he carefully prepared that way. He does not mention unessential details on the path to his goal. Whether this knowledge of French character on the part of Voltaire was carefully reasoned, or whether it was instinctive, is beyond definite proof. The fact stands that he had the knowledge. He knew the audience for which he was writing.

The passages which have been quoted from the *Histoire de Charles XII* show how penetrating was Voltaire's knowledge of political conditions throughout Europe, and how well he understood the basic qualities of freedom and liberty. His study of England was many times more thorough than his study of the countries which he treats in the *Histoire de Charles XII*, and his knowledge of English history and English institutions was much more profound than his information concerning these other nations. It seems most probable that he did understand the

English political system, for he was greatly interested in such questions. His failure to give definite evidence of this knowledge in the *Lettres Philosophiques* should not be considered conclusive proof that he lacked it.

The first shot in the seventy-year cannonade of the old régime which went on during the eighteenth century may be said to have been fired by Montesquieu in the *Lettres Persanes*. It caused much commotion, but it struck no vital spot. The second shot, which came in Voltaire's *Lettres Philosophiques*, hit home with a terrific explosion. The *Lettres Philosophiques* is, as Lytton Strachey has so succinctly put it, " the lens by means of which Voltaire gathered together the scattered rays of his English impressions into a focus of brilliant and burning intensity." In this book he communicates to the French public his discovery of England.

The *Lettres Philosophiques* is not, as it seems from a superficial point of view, a history of England. It is a criticism of France. Voltaire's personal investigation of England was widespread and impartial. The book in which he purports to give the results of this investigation is both limited and partial. In each phrase that he wrote Voltaire's one thought was as to the effect of his words upon his French readers. The book is an unparalleled monument to his ability to grasp the complicated differences of national character. He not only shows an intimate knowledge of the English and a sympathetic understanding of those racial characteristics which are usually so bewildering to the French, but he also knows every twisting by-road of French character and psychology. With the sureness of a master, with a subtlety that baffled opposition, he drove home his points. The style, the form, the content, the point of view of the book were perfectly calculated to fulfil the task it was destined to perform. Had his plan of attack been slightly different, he would have aroused an antagonism in the minds of his readers that would have defeated his purpose. Had his style not been what it was the book would never have had the wide popularity that made it so important.

The *Lettres Philosophiques* is a subtle, reasoned attack, prepared with keenest knowledge of the French character. The French were violently opposed to anything not in good taste; they were most easily won by logic and wit. The French would not have considered a direct attack upon the old régime to be in good taste. An appeal to their logic by showing the reasonableness of English institutions as compared to those of France, and to their sense of humor by showing the ridiculousness of some French customs and conventions was the surest method for Voltaire to gain his point.

The book is in the form of twenty-five letters, ostensibly written by Voltaire to his friend Thieriot, and it contains observations upon every conceivable subject. The first four letters take up what was probably to Voltaire the most striking phenomenon he saw in England — Quakerism. This faith, so diametrically opposed to Catholicism in all of its views, gave Voltaire an unexpected opportunity to attack the Church. It is easy to imagine with what gusto both clergy and laiety in France joined in laughing at the absurd habits of this austere sect — for, to one reared in the pomp of the State Church in France, the unemotional severity of the Quakers must, at first glance, have seemed

absurd. But from a logical point of view it was apparent
to every reader that right was often on the side of the
Quakers. Voltaire's humor, putting his readers off their
guard, opened a path by which his logic could enter on
its mission of destruction with deft sureness. The laugh
was at the expense of the Quakers, but the Catholics suffered the actual loss. The next three letters take up some
of the other predominant sects in England. Always seem-
ing to ridicule other faiths, Voltaire attacks the established
Church in France with methodical thoroughness. Prefacing his remarks with the statement that, " An Englishman, as a free man, goes to heaven by, whatever road
pleases him," Voltaire proceeds to show his compatriots
the elements of truth that are to be found in various sects.
He never draws the logical conclusion that Frenchmen,
too, should be free to act according to their consciences.
It is not necessary to do so.

The next three letters are titled respectively, *On Parliament*, *On Government*, and *On Commerce*, and in them
are to be found many of Voltaire's most incisive statements. Using Rome for comparison, he gives a brief account of the English government, pointing out especially
that the civil wars in England, which the French so deplored, had resulted in political liberty, while similar wars
in other countries had had no such happy results. " The
fruit of the civil wars in Rome," he says, " was slavery,
that of the turmoil in England, liberty. . . . The French
think the government of that island to be more stormy
than the sea which surrounds it, and that is true; but such
tempests arise only when the king starts them, when he
attempts to become master of a vessel on which he is

merely first mate. The civil wars in France were longer, more cruel, and more fertile in crimes than were those in England, but not one of these French wars had as its goal the obtaining of a wise and rational liberty." [17]

The book is so full of criticisms of France that it is scarcely possible to choose one passage as being more representative than another. The style of the book is so concise that one is in danger of failing to realize the importance of Voltaire's observations. In two sentences he dismisses such important topics as equal justice for rich and poor, the iniquity of the French game laws, the advantages of equal taxation, and the supremacy of the House of Commons. What other writer could convincingly discuss such topics in less than two chapters? Voltaire is so sure of himself that he is able merely to mention a thing and yet cause it to leave a vivid impression. "Here no one talks of high, intermediate, and low justice, nor of the privilege of hunting upon the property of a citizen who is not free to fire a gun upon his own domains. A man, because he is of noble birth or because he is a priest, is not exempt from taxation; all taxes are regulated by the House of Commons, which, although second in rank, is first in power." His manner of mentioning these things is in itself a discussion of them. He goes on to say, "The Lords and the Bishops are able to reject taxation bills passed by the House of Commons, but they may not change anything in them; they must either approve or reject them without qualification. When a bill is ratified by the Lords and approved by the king, everyone must pay. Each individual contributes, not according to his station in life (which is

[17] *Lettres Philosophiques*, Letter VII.

absurd), but according to his income. There is neither *taille* nor an arbitrary poll-tax, but instead, a land-tax. Under the famous king, William III, all of the estates of the country were assessed at less than their value. The tax has remained the same ever since, although the income from the lands has increased; thus no one is oppressed and no one complains. The feet of a peasant are not bruised from wearing wooden shoes, he eats white bread, he is well clothed, he is not afraid to increase the number of his cattle nor to tile his roof for fear that his taxes will be raised the ensuing year. There are many peasants here who possess two hundred thousand francs worth of goods, and who are still willing to cultivate the soil which has made them rich and on which they live in freedom." [18]

In his remarks on commerce, Voltaire brought out a point of view practically unknown in France. The French still looked upon commerce and business as degrading occupations, completely unworthy of a person with any claim to noble blood. Voltaire, with his bourgeois shrewdness, realized how vital commerce is to the welfare of any nation. He showed that the English owed their preëminent position in the world to it. " Perhaps posterity," he says, " will be surprised to learn that a small island, possessing only a small amount of lead, tin, fuller's earth, and coarse wool, became, through its commerce, powerful enough to send, in 1723, three fleets at one time to the three extremities of the world." How strikingly he contrasts the comparative usefulness to a country of war and of commerce when he says, " London was poor and rustic when Edward III conquered half of France. It is

[18] *Id.*, Letter IX.

only because the English have become merchants that London has become greater in size and in population than Paris." Voltaire's comparison of the title " English merchant " with that of " Roman citizen " must have irritated the French. But he was not content merely to irritate them; he made fun of their petty pride. " In France," he says, " anyone who wants to can become a marquis, and whoever comes to Paris from the depths of the provinces with money to spend and a name ending in *ac* or *ille,* can say, ' A man like me, a man of my position,' and haughtily disdain a merchant. The merchant hears himself and his profession scoffed at so often that he is stupid enough to be ashamed of it. And yet I am not sure which is of most use to a state, the well-powdered lord who knows the exact hour when the king arises and retires and who gives himself airs of importance while playing the rôle of a slave in the ante-chamber of a minister, or a merchant who enriches his country, who from his office gives orders in India and in Egypt, and contributes to the happiness of the world." [19]

In six letters which are devoted largely to Newton, Voltaire attempts to show the tremendous importance to the world of Newton's scientific methods and theories. Starting off with the striking pronouncement that Newton was the greatest man that the world had yet produced, Voltaire says, " If true grandeur consists in having received a powerful genius from heaven and in having used that genius for the enlightenment of oneself and of the world in general, then a man like Mr. Newton, who is to be found scarcely once in ten centuries, is the truly great man,

[19] *Id.,* Letter X.

and these politicians and conquerors, whom every century possesses, are usually nothing more than distinguished malefactors. It is to the man who dominates minds by the force of truth, not to those who make slaves by physical violence, to the man who understands the universe, not to those who disfigure it, that we owe our respect. Since you insist that I discuss the distinguished men whom England has produced, I will start with the Bacons, the Lockes, the Newtons, etc. The generals and the ministers will come in their places." [20]

Thus Voltaire took the first steps in his pursuit of this cosmopolitan ideal. No three works by a single author could vary more one from another than the *Histoire de Charles XII*, the *Essay on Epick Poetry*, and the *Lettres Philosophiques*, yet in them Voltaire was attempting, each time from a different angle, not just to bring this idea of cosmopolitanism to the attention of his compatriots, but so to impress it upon them that it would color, even direct, their minds and their lives.

[20] *Id.*, Letter XII.

CHAPTER TWELVE
CONTRASTS

CHAPTER TWELVE

CONTRASTS

To determine the influence of one man upon another, or of certain movements upon individuals, is a matter of intangible speculation. What man today can be sure of the exact influence upon his life and character of a stray excerpt from a newspaper or a chance remark overheard upon a crowded street? Many of these influences are so complex, so fragmentary, so circuitous in their effects that we ourselves are at a loss to account for them. How much more difficult, then, is an attempt two hundred years after his death to determine exactly the influences exerted upon such a complex character as that of Voltaire?

In striving for some estimate of the actual influence of England on Voltaire two facts stand out. First, there was bound to be some change in Voltaire during the period of his life which he spent in England; and second, no influence exerted upon him up to the time he left France would indicate with any sureness the nature of this change. For some time before the Rohan affair, one senses in Voltaire's letters his growing dissatisfaction with the uselessness and superficiality of the life which he was leading. Socially he had arrived at the top of the ladder. It is impossible that a man with such a capacity for accomplishment could have allowed himself to be forever engulfed in the pleasures of Parisian life. Already he was reaching out for new worlds to conquer. After the Rohan affair he was confronted with the necessity of discovering at once a new outlet for his talents. Never more could he have confidence in apparent social success.

It is interesting to speculate upon what might have attracted Voltaire's facile mind had he remained in France. He had a genius for universal knowledge and for accomplishment in almost all fields. There seems to have been almost nothing that he could not do. Would he have become a financier or a diplomat? At times he showed leanings toward both of these careers. It seems likely, that whatever he did he would have continued to write. As it happened, he was spared the necessity of a conscious choice. His future was determined by his experience in England.

Before his exile Voltaire had been largely concerned with the frills of life; when he returned from England he was deeply interested in some of the most vital problems of existence. In England for the first time his unparalleled gift of popular appeal was evoked in that tremendous struggle between " common-sense " and the powers of privilege and tradition. The significance of this fact can scarcely be exaggerated, for it was a forerunner of a new social order. The doctrine of the responsibility of the individual for his fellow followed logically from this common-sense view of society.

When Voltaire arrived in England he was a deft and superficial poet, when he left he was a " philosophe "; when he arrived in England he had the mobile inconstancy of immaturity, when he left he possessed the sureness and self-confidence of the mature man; when he arrived there his personal fortune was at a low ebb, when he left he was financially independent; when he left France social position still seemed to him one of the essential things in life, when he returned home he had risen above matters of social distinction; in the tragedies which he wrote before his exile he had used questions of politics and religion to give interest to his dramas, in those composed after his return from England he used the dramatic form to lend interest to his political opinions; in short, when he left France, Voltaire's character and the future course of his life were unformed; when he returned from England those rare particles which went to make up his unique character had crystallized into their final form. Never in after life did he do anything which, at least in part, was not influenced by this period of his life.

To a certain extent England was merely a symbol of the revolution which was occurring within Voltaire. It would be hasty to attribute the great change which came over him at this time to the influence of England alone. For Voltaire already had within himself the germs of these English influences. He had already felt, in a vague way, those things which were to burst upon him with such conviction in England. And more than that, his experiences in France had put him in a receptive mood toward them. What could have prepared him more perfectly to accept the English doctrine of political liberty than the unfortunate occurrences which preceded his exile? And what could have given a more satisfactory solution to the problem of his growing dissatisfaction with the established church in France than the common-sense doctrine of the English deists?

In the matter of religion, especially, did the sudden

contrast of England to France decide the course of Voltaire's life. Before he left France his belief in the Church had been severely undermined by the French philosophers, but, as we have seen, they had not succeeded in breaking down entirely his somewhat instinctive faith in the religion of his childhood. The influence of Bayle and of his own contemporaries would very likely have made Voltaire a freethinker, but, as it actually happened, his attacks upon the Church were based upon those of the English deists. In England the matter-of-fact viewpoint of the rationalists struck him with tremendous force, and he finally realized that he had never possessed any real faith in the Catholic Church. Throughout the rest of his life Voltaire's scepticism, like that of his friend Bolingbroke, was based on common-sense.

The foundations of Voltaire's deism were laid by Descartes, Bayle, and Fontenelle; his final conversion was brought about by the English deists — Herbert, Shaftesbury, Toland, Collins, Woolston, Tindal, and Bolingbroke —all of whom influenced him. From Shaftesbury he borrowed the doctrine of the inherent goodness of man, which he often invoked against the Christian doctrine of original sin.[1] It is undoubted that Toland's *Christianity Not Mysterious* influenced him. Voltaire's attacks upon the ethics of the Scriptures were based upon those of Tindal, who was one of the first persons to note the immoral nature of some of the commands of Jehovah and of many of the acts of the patriarchs and the prophets. We also find

---

[1] It is interesting to note that in his preface to the *Poème sur le désastre de Lisbonne* Voltaire is the first person to call attention to the fact that Pope's philosophy is borrowed entirely from Shaftesbury. Moland, *Oeuvres de Voltaire*, Vol. XXII, p. 177 f.

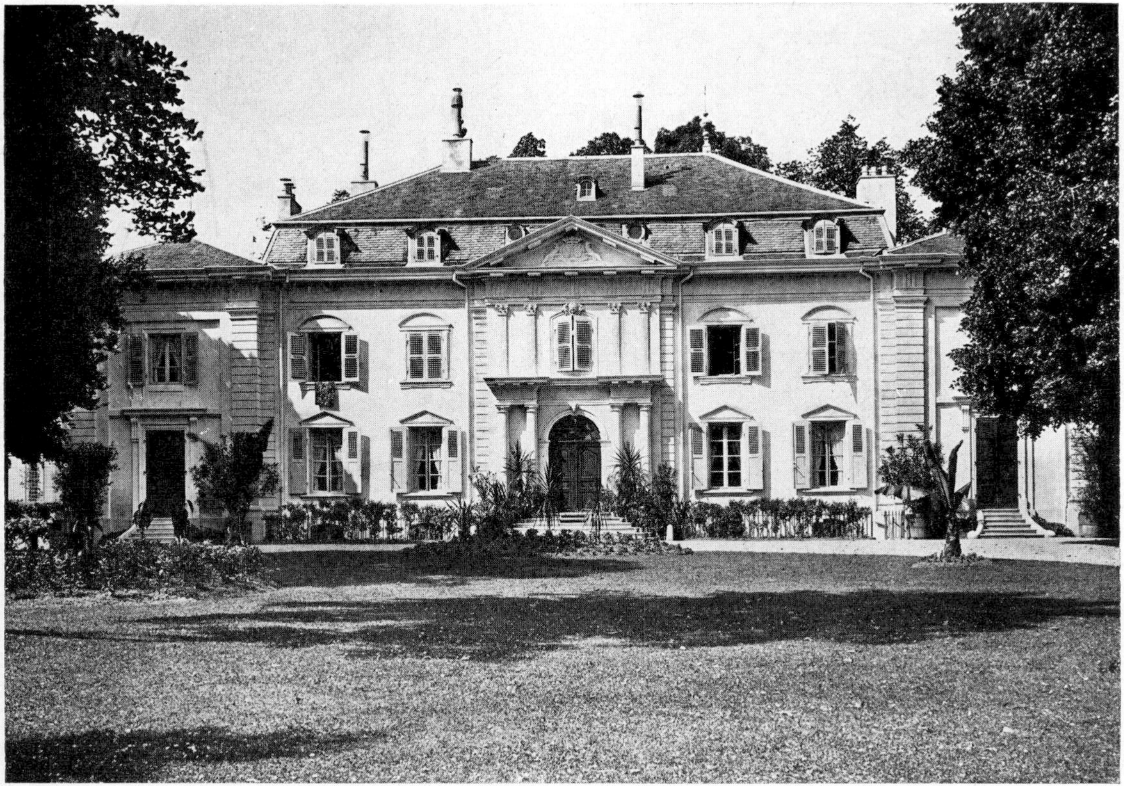

Voltaire's Château at Ferney

in Tindal the hatred for the Jews and the tenderness for the Chinese that we find in Voltaire.

It is interesting to note that the one English philosopher whose disciple Voltaire claimed to be, had little influence upon him. Voltaire knew Locke in England, and claimed to be his disciple, but, at bottom, they had little in common except an aversion for metaphysics. As Warburton once said, " Locke took men to the door of free thought, but he did not open the door of it for them." It was this door that Voltaire, inspired by what he had seen in England, wanted to leave open for ever.

Leslie Stephen says of Voltaire, " He left England after imbibing from the English deists the principles which, stored up in his keen intelligence, were to be radiated forth in the shape of the keenest of all human sarcasms, and to precipitate in helpless mist the cloudy structures of old superstition. That arch iconoclast appears to have studied with lively sympathy and turned to good account in his own writings the arguments put forth in Tindal's *Christianity as Old as Creation.*" [2]

The determination of the exact influence upon Voltaire of individual English deists is beyond the scope of this work. One is not even sure whether a detailed differentiation between the influences of these various men is to be desired. The influences at work during this period of Voltaire's life are so complex that it is almost impossible to make definite statements about individual details with precision. One is safe in saying, however, that Voltaire's final philosophy and his mature attitude toward religion were determined by the influences of the English deists,

[2] Stephen, *English Thought in the Eighteenth Century*, Vol. III, p. 43.

falling upon ground prepared by the French philosophers. Theoretically, there can be found in the unaided influence of French thinkers enough material for the determination of Voltaire's philosophic views; actually, his philosophy of life was fixed by the overwhelming flood of ideas, propounded by the English deists, with which he came into contact during his exile. And the determination of Voltaire's philosophy was one of the most important events in that exciting period, the eighteenth century; for what Voltaire thought and what he wrote were destined to be the bases for the thoughts and the intimate writings of the most influential portion of eighteenth century society in France, and, indeed, in much of Europe.

It is well known that Voltaire's writings were in large part responsible for the popularity of eighteenth century French philosophy. What is not so generally recognized is that in England was at least developed, if, indeed, it did not originate there, that quality in his literary style which was to such a degree responsible for the popularity of his writings and for the ready acceptance of his conclusions. The distinguishing mark of the eighteenth century in France was philosophy; the unusual thing about this philosophy was its popular acceptance; the reason for its acceptance was that it was put forth in short, spicy, interesting books. The *Lettres Philosophiques* was the first book in which this original combination was attempted, and in this fact, rather than in the illuminating subject-matter of the book, lies its deep significance.

When Voltaire started the *Lettres Philosophiques* he had before him the problem of discovering a literary medium by means of which he might express convincingly, yet attractively, the reactions about conditions in France which his acquaintance with England had given him. The problem was complex. Writing as he was with the hope of influencing an appreciable number of his fellow-countrymen, his book must have wide appeal and it must be amusing. Yet to treat of the subjects necessitated by his plan he must discuss questions as widely varied as theology and politics, commerce and philosophy, vaccination and literature; he must acquaint his compatriots with Bacon and with Locke, and bring clearly to their minds the importance of Newton's intricate scientific theories. And at the same time the book was to be a series of running comments upon conditions in France! Granted that Voltaire wrote for an audience of far greater intelligence than that of most writers today, even so, what a problem was before him in attempting to weld such weighty subjects together into a book which was both to be a " best seller " and which was also to influence profoundly serious thought throughout the country! And in addition he was forced to beware of the activity of the official censor, so dangerous to any writer in France.

To meet these needs was evolved that rhythmic, concise, brilliant, witty, " typically French " style that was Voltaire's in his mature years. Never has a writer possessed a means of literary expression so completely adapted to his personality, to his ability, and to the particular necessities of his own type of writing as was Voltaire's style. It allowed the treatment of the widest variety of subjects while calling into play those qualities with which his genius was most richly endowed. It allowed him to be serious, witty, entertaining, and didactic, all in one breath.

No one could claim that a style so evidently suited to the genius of a great writer was due primarily to the influence of a foreign country, yet the fact remains that this style was developed in England to meet the new intellectual needs which Voltaire's experience in England had developed. Had Voltaire never gone to England it seems at least doubtful whether he would ever have achieved this form of expression. Moreover, there are distinct traces of the influence of Swift in this new style of Voltaire's. Especially in such a literary trick as the characterization of a social institution or function by the description of some external act connected with it did he borrow from Swift, as, for instance, " nous ne pensons pas que le christianisme consiste à jeter de l'eau froide sur la tête, avec un peu de sel," or, " des meutriers vetus de rouge avec un bonnet haut de deux pieds, enrolant des citoyens en faisant du bruit avec deux petits batons sur une peau d'ane bien tendue." [3] But rather than in the actual imitation of some of Swift's literary mannerisms, Voltaire's entire style in the *Lettres Philosophiques* seems reminiscent of and perhaps colored by Swift. His clear, keen, exact sentences, his deft, ironic sarcasm, his mocking similes, his instant perception of the ludicrous, his shrewd estimate of values, while they are all undoubted qualities of Voltaire himself, are expressed so much more stimulatingly than ever before that one feels that Voltaire must have found real inspiration in the prose of the great Irish Dean while he was forming his own peerless style.

It is easy to point out that this or that in England had

[3] M. Baldensperger, *op. cit.*, p. 371, calls attention to this influence of Swift upon Voltaire.

great influence upon Voltaire. It is hard, however, to show how great was the total effect upon him of the contrast of England to France. Before Voltaire left France he was like an artist working at an intricate mosaic without a copy of the design before him. The design was the plan of his life. When he got to England he was able to get some distance away from it, to see it in perspective, and, at once, everything became surprisingly simple. Insignificant detail dropped away in a flash, leaving the important curves and angles startling in their direct clarity. Henceforth it was his task to complete the design here glimpsed.

In England, for the first time in his life, Voltaire found a definite standard by which to weigh and judge his native land. He found a different point of view, and people with different prejudices and different conventions. Judging from the point of view of abstract right and wrong, it had been impossible for Voltaire to differentiate between solid truths and the mere conventions upon which he had been reared. He had vaguely felt incongruities in his beliefs, but he had possessed no standard for comparison. All had been abstract. Here at last was a concrete basis for contrast. At one glance he saw the absurd provincialism of the French attitude when they pretended to ignore as unworthy of attention anything not French. He realized the restrictions in the highly formulated and stilted French life. He saw a lack of vitality in their precious elegance, and a lack of sincerity in their stylized religion. Out of a jumbled heap of prejudices and half-felt beliefs came the sure distinction between significant and insignificant, the final conviction as to the ends of life.

The contrast of England to France was the conclusive

test-by-fire of all of Voltaire's early theories and instincts. It was the final formative influence of his life; in England were definitely determined his future aims and ambitions.

It is true that many distinguished writers, after studying Voltaire's life, have felt that it was the discipline of his scientific study during his residence at Cirey which wrought in him that remarkable metamorphosis in which he changed from a superficial poet to a philosophic encyclopedist and an exponent of cosmopolitanism. But to one who realizes fully the influence upon him of his visit to England, such a position is scarcely tenable. It was the new point of view gained in England which caused him to submit to the restraint and study of Cirey.

The *Lettres Philosophiques* was Voltaire's first public exhibition of this new point of view and of his new ambitions. It was his declaration of war upon the old régime. Then, instead of continuing the battle here started, he spent fifteen years with Mme. du Châtelet at Cirey. This experience built up for him a wide reputation as a serious and solid thinker. His connection with Frederick the Great gilded the dome of notoriety which his experiments at Cirey had built. Then, fully equipped, he retired to Ferney to resume the great battle.

BIBLIOGRAPHY

Les *Annalles Politiques et Littéraires* (1916), Lanson: *La prose de Voltaire.*

Archiv für das Studium der Neueven Sprachen . . . 1913, Baldensperger: *La Chronologie du séjour de Voltaire en Angleterre.*

Athenaeum, December, 1893; January, 1913.

Baldensperger, *Études d'histoire littéraire,* 2e sèrie.

Ballantyne, *Voltaire's Visit to England.*

Barclay, R., *Theologiae vere Christiannae Appologia* (1675).

Baretti, *Discours sur Shakespeare et sur M. de Voltaire.*

Baudrillart, *Discours sur Voltaire.*

Beaune, *Voltaire au Collège.*

Beljame, *Le public et les hommes de lettres en Angleterre au XVIIIe Siècle.*

Bengesco, *Voltaire, Bibliographie de ses Oeuvres.*

Bersot, *Études.*

Bertaut, J., *Voltaire.*

Berville, *Les premières amours de Voltaire.*

Beuchot, *Oeuvres Complètes de Voltaire.*

Bloch, L., *La Philosophie de Newton.*

Bolingbroke, *Lettres Historiques, Politiques, etc.*

Bonnefou, *Voltaire et J-B. Rousseau,* Revue d'Histoire Littéraire de la France.

Boury, *Voltaire et l'Italie.*

British Gazeteer, The,

British Journal, The,

Brunetière, *Études critiques.*

——, *L'Évolution des Genres dans l'Histoire de la littérature française.*

Byron, *Journal.*

Carlyle, *History of Frederick the Great.*

Caussy, *Lettres inédites de Voltaire à Thieriot*, Revue d'Histoire Lit. de la France.

Champion, *Voltaire — Études Critiques.*

Charlane, *L'Influence Français en Angleterre.*

Châteauneuf, *Les Divorces Anglais.*

Chetwood, W. R., *A General History of the Stage.*

Clogenson, *La Vie de Voltaire.*

Colini, *Mon séjour auprès de Voltaire.*

Collet, *Relics of Literature.*

Collins, J. C., *Voltaire in England.*

Condorcet, *Vie de Voltaire.*

Coulon, *Le fidèle conducteur pour le voyage d'Angleterre.*

Craftsman, The (London).

Croft, *Life of Young.*

Daily Courant (London).

Daily Journal, The (London).

Daily Post (London).

Delort, J., *Histoire de la Détention des Philosophes.*

Dennis, J., *On the Genius and Writings of Shakespeare.*

De Saussure, *Letters.*

Desfontaines, Abbé G., *La Voltairomanie.*

Desnoiresterres, *Voltaire et la Société Française.*

De Witt, Cornélis, *La Société française et la société anglaise au XVIIIᵉ Siècle.*

Dryden, J., *Works*, ed. Scott-Saintsbury.

Dubois, Raymond, *Voltaire comme homme de science.*

le Duc, L., *Voltaire et la police.*

Duvernet, *Vie de Voltaire.*

Elwin, *Pope.*

English Review, The (February, 1914).

Examen important de milord Bolingbroke (Geneva, 1767).

Faguet, *Amours d'hommes de letters, Voltaire.*

——, *Politique comparée de Montesquieu, J-J. Rousseau et Voltaire.*

——, *Voltaire.*

——, *XVIIIe Siècle.*

Flying Post (or *Weekly Medley*), October, 1728 ff.

Fontaine, L., *Le Théâtre et la Philosophie au XVIIIe Siècle.*

Fosse, de la, *Manlius.*

Foulet, *Correspondance de Voltaire 1726–1729.*

Funck-Brentano, *Voltaire . . . et les lettres de Cachet.*

Gasté, *Voltaire à Caen en 1713.*

Gastineau, *Voltaire en exile.*

Genlis, Mme. la Comtesse de, *Mémoires sur le XVIIIe Siècle.*

Gentleman's Magazine, June, 1732; February, 1747; November, 1758; October, 1797.

Goldsmith, O., *Life of Voltaire.*

de Goncourt, J., *Love in the XVIIIth Century.*

Grafigny, Mme. de, *Vie Privée de Voltaire et de Mme. du Châtelet.*

Graham, *Annals and Correspondence of the First and Second Earls of Stair.*

Haines, C. M., *Shakespeare in France, Criticism, Voltaire to Victor Hugo.*

Hampstead Annual, The, 1903, Hales, J. W., *Voltaire in Hampstead.*

Harvey-St. John, *Bolingbroke.*

Havens, G. R., *The Abbé Prévost and English Literature.*

Hémon, F., *Cours de Littérature*, vols. VI and VII.

Historical Memoirs of the Author of the Henriade.

Houssage, *Le Roi Voltaire.*

Howard, *Collection of Letters.*

Huchon, *Mrs. Montagu and Her Friends.*

Hurn, A. S., *Voltaire et Bolingbroke.*

Johnson, *Life of Pope.*

Journal des Sçavans, 1728.

Jullemier, *Voltaire Capitaliste.*

Jusserand, J. J., *English Essays from a French Pen.*

——, *Shakespeare en France sous l'ancien régime.*

Kervan, Armel de, *Voltaire, ses hontes, ses crimes,* etc.

Laclos, *Liaisons dangereuses.*

Lacombe, *La Poétique de Voltaire.*

Lanfrey, *L'Église et les Philosophes au XVIIIᵉ Siècle.*

Lanson, G., *Bibliographie de l'Histoire de Littérature.*

——, *L'Art de Prose.*

——, *Voltaire.*

——, *Voltaire et son banquéroutier juif, La Revue Latine,* 1908.

——, *Voltaire et l'Affaire des Lettres Anglaises, Revue de Paris,* 1904.

——, *Voltaire et les Lettres Philosophiques, Revue de Paris,* 1908.

——, *Voltaire, Les Lettres Philosophiques* (edition).

Lavisse, *Histoire de France.*

Legrange-Chancel, *Philippiques.*

Lion, H., *Les tragédies . . . de Voltaire.*

Longchamp et Wagnière, *Oeuvres de Voltaire.*

Lounsbury, *Voltaire and Shakespeare.*

Lowndes, W. T., *The Bibliographer's Manual.*

Macdonald, F., *Studies in the France of Voltaire and Rousseau.*

Marias, *Journal et Mémoires.*

Martin, H., *Voltaire et Rousseau et la philosophie du XVIIIᵉ Siècle.*

Martin, L., *Esprit de Voltaire.*

Maty, *Memoires of Chesterfield.*

Maugras, G., *La Cour de Lunéville au XVIIIᵉ Siècle.*

——, *Quarelles des Philosophes, Voltaire et Rousseau.*

Mémoires du Président Henault.

Mémoires inédites de Mme. la Comtesse de Genlis.

Mémoires pour servir à la Vie de M. V.

Mercure de France, 1728.

Milton, J., *Poetical Works,* ed. D. Masson.

Modern Language Revue, Robertson, J. G., *The Knowledge of Shakespeare on the Continent at the beginning of the XVIIIth Century,* 1925.

Moland, *Oeuvres de Voltaire.*

Molinar, *Lettres Servant de Réponse aux Lettres Philosophiques.*

Monsieur de Voltaire peinte par lui-même, 1769.

Montagu, Mrs. E., *An Essay on the Writings and the Genius of Shakespeare.* (Dublin, 1769.)

Morley, C., *Voltaire.*

National Review, August, 1892.

Nichol, *Literary Anecdotes of the Eighteeth Century.*

Nicolardot, L., *Ménage et Finances de Voltaire.*

Niscard, *Les ennemies de Voltaire.*

Noel, *Voltaire, sa Vie et ses Oeuvres.*

Notes and Queries, First Series. *Major Brome's visit to Voltaire.*

Northcote, J., *Life of Sir Joshua Reynolds.*

Nourisson, *Voltaire et la Voltairianisme.*

Oeuvres Universitaire, 1921. *Un Carnet de Notes de Voltaire.*

Otway, *Venice Preserved.*

Parton, *The Life of Voltaire.*

Peignot, *Recherches sur les ouvrages de Voltaire.*

Pellissier, *Voltaire Philosophe.*

Perrault, C., *Parallèle des Anciens et des Modernes.* (1692.)

Phillmore, *Lyttelton.*

Pierron, A., *Voltaire et ses Maîtres.*

Polnitz, *Mémoires.*

Pope, *Preface to an Edition of Shakespeare.*

Present State of the Republic of Letters, The.

Prévost-Leygonie, *La Jeunesse de Voltaire.*

Quérard, *Écrits relatifs aux ouvrages et à la personne de Voltaire.*

Rapin, R., *Réflexions sur la Poétique.* (1675.)

Rémuset, C., *L'Angleterre au XVIIIᵉ Siècle.*

Renard, *Vie de Voltaire.*

Revue des Deux Mondes, November, 1889, Brunetière, *l'Influence de l'Angleterre sur Voltaire.*

Review, The English, February, 1914, *A Notebook of Voltaire's in England.*

Revue d'Histoire Littéraire de la France; 1894. Texte, *Origines du Cosmopolitanisme littéraire au XVIIIᵉ Siècle.*

——, 1902, Bonnefou, *Voltaire et J. B. Rousseau.*

——, 1906, 1908. Foulet, *Le Voyage de Voltaire en Angleterre.*

——, 1909, Caussy, *Lettres inédites de Voltaire à Thieriot.*

Revue Historique, 1908, Sée, H., *Les idées politiques de Voltaire.*

Revue Latine, 1908, Lanson, *Voltaire et son banquéroutier juif en Angleterre.*

Richmond, L. de, *Après le Révocation de l'Édict de Nantes: Voltaire et la liberté de Conscience, Annale de l'Académie de La Rochelle*, 1885.

Rigault, H., *Histoire de la Quarelle des Ancienes et des Modernes.*

Ritter, E., *Voltaire et le Pasteur Robert Brown*, Bulletin de la Société de l'Histoire du Protestantisme français, 1904.

Robert, L., *Voltaire et l'intolérance religieuse.*

Roberts, W., *Memoires of the Life and Correspondence of Mrs. Hannah Moore.*

Robertson, *The Knowledge of Shakespeare on the Continent.*

Rólli P., *Remarks upon M. Voltaire's Essay on the Epick Poetry of the European Nations.* (London, 1728.)

Ruffhead, *Life of Pope.*

Saigey, *Les Sciences au XVIIIᵉ Siècle; — La Phisique de Voltaire.*

Saint-Hyacinthe, *Lettres Critiques sur le Henriade.* (London, 1728.)

Saintsbury, G., *A History of Criticism.*

Sayous, *Le XVIIIᵉ Siècle à l'Étranger.*

Sée, H., *Les idées politiques de Voltaire.*

Seward, *Anecdotes of Distinguished Persons.*

Shaftesbury, *Advice to an Author*, Part II.

Sichel, W., *Bolingbroke and his Times.*

Spectator, ed. Morley.

Spence, J., *Anecdotes and Observations, and Character of Books and Men.*

Spingarn, J., *A History of Literary Criticism in the Renaissance.*

Stephen, L., *English Thought in the Eighteenth Century.*

Strachey, L., *Books and Characters.*

Swift, J., *Works.*

Tabarand, *Histoire Critique du Philosophisme Anglais.*

—— , *De la Philosophie de la Henriade.*

Taine, *L'Ancien Régime.*

Tallentyre, *Life of Voltaire.*

Taylor, J., *Memoires.*

Texte, J., *J-J. Rousseau et le Cosmopolitisme littéraire.*

Villemain, *Tableau de la littérature au XVIIIᵉ Siècle.*

Walpole, H., *Letters*, ed. Mrs. Toynbee.

Warburton, *Letters.*

Weekly Journal, The (London).

White, F. D., *Voltaire's Essay on Epic Poetry.*

Whorton, *Pope.*

Williams, F., *Memoires and Correspondence of Bishop Atterbury.*

INDEX